The Access to Neighbouring Land Act Handbook

Written by

Tina Matthews, FILEX

Edited by

Victor H Vegoda FRICS IRRV FBEng PEng MEWI

Number 12
in the "Need to Know" Series

Copies of Acts of Parliament and Explanatory notes reproduced by the kind permission of Her Majesty's Stationery Office

Grateful thanks to Estates Gazette and to The Incorporated Council of Law Reporting for England and Wales for permission to reproduce their law reports

Thanks to Alistair Redler for making available to the author material on the case of *Coulton v Pickles*

Published in February 2003

ISBN **1 898383 75 8**

DISCLAIMER

Great care has been taken in producing this book but neither the writer, editor, publishers nor anyone associated with this book will accept responsibility for problems arising from its use — no matter how arising.

Other Titles in the "Need to Know" Series:-

Practical Ways to Recover Your Debts
A Practical Guide to Residential Surveys
Schedules of Dilapidations
Heave Demolition and Reconstruction
Draft Your Own Terms of Engagement
Condam — Draft Your Own Safety Plan
Landlord & Tenant Covenants Act, 1995
An Introduction to the Party Wall etc. Act 1996
Contract (Rights of Third Parties) Act 1999
Liability of the Negligent Surveyor
The Dilapidations Handbook

CONTENTS

Chapter 1	Purpose of this book	5
Chapter 2	The position prior to the Access to Neighbouring Land Act 1992	7
Chapter 3	History of the Access to Neighbouring Land Act 1992	11
Chapter 4	A word of caution to the conveyancing lawyer	13
Chapter 5	Section 1 - Access Orders	15
Chapter 6	Section 2 - Terms and conditions of Access Orders	25
Chapter 7	Section 3 - Effect of Access Order	37
Chapter 8	Section 4 - Persons bound by Access Order, unidentified persons and bar on contracting out	45
Chapter 9	Section 5 - Registration of Access Orders and of applications for such orders	51
Chapter 10	Section 6 - Variation of Orders and damages for breach	57
Chapter 11	Section 7 - Jurisdiction over, and allocation of, proceedings	59
Chapter 12	Section 8 - Interpretation and application	61
Chapter 13	Section 9 - Short title, commencement and extent	63

APPENDICES

Statutes:

1. Access to Neighbouring Land Act 1992 65
2. Extract from the Law of Property Act 1925 – Section 62 81
3. Extracts from the Law Commission Report No. 151 on Rights of Access to Neighbouring Land 83
4. Copy of Order 49 – Rule 1 of the County Court Supplementary Rules (information to be included in an application for an Access Order) 93

5. Definitions/interpretations 95

6. **Checklists** 103
   Applicant's Checklist 103
   Respondent's Checklist 108

7. **Cases brought under the Access to Neighbouring Land Act 1992** 113
   Dean v Walker 1996 113
   Coulton v Pickles 1995 116
   Williams v Edwards and Edwards 1997 119

8. **How to find out more information about the servient land** 121

9. **Precedents:** 123
   Precedent for an application for an Access Order 123
   Precedent for an answer agreeing to the making of an Order but specifying terms 127
   Precedent for an answer objecting to an Access Order 129
   Precedent for an application to vary the terms of an Access Order 131
   Precedent for a claim for damages for breach of an Access Order 133

10. **Selected extracts from relevant cases** 135

TABLE OF STATUTES 197
TABLE OF CASES 203
INDEX 207

Chapter 1

Purpose of this book

The Access to Neighbouring Land Act 1992 ("ANLA") was introduced to assist in situations where a landowner needs to repair part of his property, but has to enter upon his neighbour's land in order to do so, and that neighbour will not consent. If a successful action is brought under this Act the neighbour seeking the access *"the applicant"* will be granted an Access Order, for a specified period of time, against the wishes of his neighbour *"the respondent"*. There is no automatic right to an Access Order under the Act.

My aim in writing this book is to guide readers through the trials and tribulations of the ANLA, but let me say at the very outset that the ANLA should only be used as a last resort.

An application under the ANLA will be time consuming and expensive, and there is no absolute guarantee that the courts will grant the access being sought. The success or failure of negotiations for access will depend to a great extent on how the initial request is made.

Human nature being what it is, a request from one neighbour to another along the following lines *"let me onto your land or I'll take you to court"* is unlikely to elicit a favourable response. In all probability that neighbour will simply dig his heals in and refuse access. It is therefore important to set off on the right foot. A polite request for access from one friendly neighbour to another will rarely be refused. It is far better to live in harmony with one's neighbours rather than to threaten them with court proceedings.

If you happen to be the person seeking access I would strongly advocate that you bend over backwards to reach agreement with your neighbour and thus avoid putting yourself in a situation where your only option is an application under the ANLA with no guarantee that an Access Order will be granted. Even if an Access Order is granted it will only provide for access to your neighbour's property for one specified period of time. Do not forget that you may require access again at a later date. If you have antagonised your neighbour it is highly unlikely that he will consent to access on a second occasion and you will have to go back to court again for another Access Order.

This book can be used in respect of access to all types of neighbouring property, whether residential or commercial. But because disputes involving residential property tend to impinge on the emotions of residents and owners, they naturally bear a higher risk of giving rise to festering feuds between neighbours. It is hoped that this book will contribute - at least in some way - to the avoidance or amelioration of such disputes.

Chapter 2

The position prior to the Access to Neighbouring Land Act 1992

Prior to the Access to Neighbouring Land Act 1992 it was of course always possible to go on to your neighbour's land with his permission. For that matter it was possible to enter upon your neighbour's land without his permission, as a trespasser, and bear the consequences if your unauthorised entry was discovered. Your neighbour over whose land you required access could also ask you to pay him a sum of money for the privilege of entering onto his land to maintain your property. Whilst this may be un-neighbourly this scenario was quite common and worked as long as the sum of money required was reasonable. If an unreasonable sum was demanded there was absolutely nothing that could be done about it. The neighbour requiring the access either had to "put up or shut up". The legal system could not intervene and help in these circumstances. It was this scenario, which in part, led to the Access to Neighbouring Land Act 1992.

Access to your neighbour's land may also have existed as an easement. Easements can be acquired in numerous ways. They can be: -

Methods of acquiring an easement:

Express grant of easement by deed

These express easements are to be found mainly in conveyancing transactions relating to residential developments and in commercial leases. There may be a clause in the conveyancing documentation relating to your property giving you a right to use a pathway belonging to your neighbour, and that will be the extent of your right over your neighbour's land. A right of way will not give you the right to bring ladders or other equipment onto your neighbour's land or the right to remain there for several days while you carry out repair work to your own property.

Presumed grant of easement - acquisition by prescription

An easement can be obtained by prescription. A right can sometimes be acquired if it has been used for at least 20 years. Once you have been using, for example, a right of way over your neighbour's land for at least 20 years, only your neighbour, as the landowner, can put a stop to it. Once you have used the right for 40 years or more it cannot be taken away from you. Part of the criteria required to prove that a right has been acquired by prescription is to show that the right has been used regularly and without the consent of the landowner. I can find no cases to indicate that an easement by prescription has ever been held to exist giving a person the right to go on to his neighbours' land for the purpose of repairing his own property. It would no doubt be difficult to prove that entry upon the neighbours' land had been a regular occurrence and without the neighbours' consent. The odd visit to your neighbours' land for maintenance purposes would be insufficient.

Doctrine of lost modern grant and The Prescription Act 1832 as means of acquiring an easement

A presumed grant can also be obtained under the doctrine of lost modern grant or under the Prescription Act 1832 but these are rare.

Implied right of access

Section 62 of the Law of Property Act 1925 implies into every conveyance of a legal estate in land, a number of rights to which the new owner shall be entitled, unless these have been specifically excluded. An extract of this section of the Law of Property Act is set out in Appendix 2.

Right of way of necessity

There is also a right of way of necessity if land is land-locked and there is the rule in *Wheeldon v Burrows*. There are also *equitable easements* and *quasi-easements* but a detailed discussion of these is outside the scope of this book.

By statute

An easement may be granted by Act of Parliament. For example giving a utility company the right to lay and maintain underground pipes.

The London Building Acts

The London Building Acts also give a right to go on to your neighbours' land in very limited circumstances providing the land is situated within the London area.

The position at common law

There is no general common law right to enter upon your neighbour's land to make repairs to your own property no matter how vital these repairs are to you, or how minimal the disturbance will be to your neighbour.

The Access to Neighbouring Land Act was introduced to provide a remedy to persons seeking access to a neighbouring property to carry out necessary repairs to their own property, and who had been refused access by their neighbour. The Act does not create a right of access, as such, but gives the person seeking access to his neighbours' land, the right to go to court and obtain an Access Order in certain circumstances.

Chapter 3

History of the Access to Neighbouring Land Act 1992

On the 3rd August 1978 the issues surrounding access to neighbouring land were referred by the Lord Chancellor to the Law Commission under the Law Commissions Act 1965. The Lord Chancellor's Department had been approached by members of the public and Members of Parliament regarding difficulties caused by lack of access. The Lord Chancellor asked the Law Commissions *"to consider the legal difficulties of those who, lacking the legal right to do so, need to enter upon another's land in order to inspect or do work upon their own, to consider whether these difficulties can be remedied by legislation and to make recommendations."*

On the 13th August 1980 the Law Commission prepared their Working Paper No. 78 on the Rights of Access to Neighbouring Land which was circulated to relevant authorities and other interested parties for comment and criticism.

A pamphlet summarising the main issues discussed in the working paper was also available. The working paper received extensive coverage in the press and on the radio and television, as the topic was one of general public interest. The Law Commission received a good response to the working paper. The majority of those who responded were in favour of a change in the law to enable a landowner a right of access to neighbouring land for the purpose of repairing or maintaining his own property. However this was subject to the view in many cases that to quote an old maxim "an Englishman's home is his castle". It was clear from the views of the majority who responded to the working paper that the neighbour should also be afforded some protection if there was a change in the law.

This working paper gave a very straightforward illustration of the problem they were trying to resolve as follows:-

Chapter 3 — History of the Access to Neighbouring Land Act 1992

"X and Y are adjoining landowners. X's house is built very close to the boundary with Y's land. It needs repair and some of the repairs can be carried out only if X (or his builders) can obtain access to the flank wall by entering Y's land for this purpose and Y will not let him do so. The result may be that X's house falls inevitably into increasing disrepair."

The working paper expressed the provisional view that the law should be altered so as to enable landowners to have some general means of obtaining access to neighbouring land to do work on their own property.

Several years went by and in December 1985 the Law Commission published their Report No. 151 on the Rights of Access to Neighbouring Land which had a draft bill annexed to it.

The matter again lay dormant for a few more years, and in 1991 a backbench Member of Parliament was stirred into action, no doubt by a member of his constituency, and introduced a private members' bill in almost identical terms to the draft bill annexed to the Law Commission Report No. 151. The draft bill went through parliament, followed a couple of weeks later by a short debate in the House of Lords. This draft bill came in for heavy criticism and was generally regarded as unworkable and it was allowed to lapse.

Towards the end of 1991 an amended bill was put before the House of Lords and was debated in the early part of 1992. This amended bill, accompanied by other bills, was then rushed through parliament before the general election and was given the Royal Assent on the 16th March 1992.

Date Act came into force

The Act came into force on the 31st January 1993.

Chapter 4

A word of caution to the conveyancing lawyer

As all conveyancing lawyers will know The Council of Mortgage Lenders Handbook was published in July 1999. Since the Handbook was published it has been amended, and a Second Edition came into effect on the 1st October 2002. Over 100 mortgage providers have now adopted this handbook. Section 6.8.1 of the handbook relates to easements and states: -

"You must take all reasonable steps to check that the property has the benefit of all easements necessary for its full use and enjoyment. This would include, for example, rights of way (both vehicular and pedestrian), the use of services and any necessary right of entry for repair. All such rights must be enforceable by the borrower and the borrower's successors in title. If they are not, you must report to us."

In the absence of an easement giving the necessary rights of entry for repair, over a neighbouring property, some lawyers are, quite rightly, reporting this defect in the title to their client and the mortgage provider. However some of these lawyers then go on to suggest that if ever there was a problem, the Access to Neighbouring Land Act 1992, would provide the solution.

As will be seen from the contents of this book an application for an Access Order under the Access to Neighbouring Land Act 1992 is fraught with difficulties, and the outcome of an application is by no means certain. In limited circumstances it may assist a client if in the future, that client has problems with his neighbour over access. However no lawyer is in a position to guarantee that an Access Order will be granted, as each individual case will be decided by the court on its own merits. This should be made clear to the client and the mortgage provider.

In this day and age a lawyer must be careful to protect his client's interests and his own reputation.

Chapter 5

Section 1: Access Orders

1 (1) A person-

(a) who, for the purpose of carrying out works to any land (the "dominant land"), desires to enter upon any adjoining or adjacent land (the "servient land"), and
(b) who needs, but does not have, the consent of some other person to that entry, may make an application to the court for an order under this section ("an Access Order") against that other person.

(2) On an application under this section, the court shall make an Access Order if, and only if, it is satisfied-

(a) that the works are reasonably necessary for the preservation of the whole or any part of the dominant land; and
(b) that they cannot be carried out, or would be substantially more difficult to carry out, without entry upon the servient land;

but this subsection is subject to subsection (3) below.

(3) The court shall not make an Access Order in any case where it is satisfied that, were it to make such an order-

(a) the respondent or any other person would suffer interference with, or disturbance of, his use or enjoyment of the servient land, or
(b) the respondent, or any other person (whether of full age or capacity or not) in occupation of the whole or any part of the servient land, would suffer hardship, to such a degree by reason of the entry (notwithstanding any requirement of

this Act or any term or condition that may be imposed under it) that it would be unreasonable to make the order.

(4) Where the court is satisfied on an application under this section that it is reasonably necessary to carry out any basic preservation works to the dominant land, those works shall be taken for the purposes of this Act to be reasonably necessary for the preservation of the land; and in this subsection "basic preservation works" means any of the following, that is to say-

(a) the maintenance, repair or renewal of any part of a building or other structure comprised in, or situate on, the dominant land;

(b) the clearance, repair or renewal of any drain, sewer, pipe or cable so comprised or situate;

(c) the treatment, cutting back, felling, removal or replacement of any hedge, tree, shrub or other growing thing which is so comprised and which is, or is in danger of becoming, damaged, diseased, dangerous, insecurely rooted or dead;

(d) the filling in, or clearance, of any ditch so comprised;

but this subsection is without prejudice to the generality of the works which may, apart from it, be regarded by the court as reasonably necessary for the preservation of any land.

(5) If the court considers it fair and reasonable in all the circumstances of the case, works may be regarded for the purposes of this Act as being reasonably necessary for the preservation of any land (or, for the purposes of subsection (4) above, as being basic preservation works which it is reasonably

necessary to carry out to any land) notwithstanding that the works incidentally involve-

(a) the making of some alteration, adjustment or improvement to the land, or
(b) the demolition of the whole or any part of a building or structure comprised in or situate upon the land.

(6) Where any works are reasonably necessary for the preservation of the whole or any part of the dominant land, the doing to the dominant land of anything which is requisite for, incidental to, or consequential on, the carrying out of those works shall be treated for the purposes of this Act as the carrying out of works which are reasonably necessary for the preservation of that land; and references in this Act to works, or to the carrying out of works, shall be construed accordingly.

(7) Without prejudice to the generality of subsection (6) above, if it is reasonably necessary for a person to inspect the dominant land-

(a) for the purpose of ascertaining whether any works may be reasonably necessary for the preservation of the whole or any part of that land,
(b) for the purpose of making any map or plan, or ascertaining the course of any drain, sewer, pipe or cable, in preparation for, or otherwise in connection with, the carrying out of works which are so reasonably necessary, or
(c) otherwise in connection with the carrying out of any such works, the making of such an inspection shall be taken for the purposes of this Act to be the carrying out to the dominant land of works which are reasonably necessary for the preservation of that land; and references in this Act to

works, or to the carrying out of works, shall be construed accordingly.

OBSERVATIONS ON SECTION 1:

No automatic or absolute right to an Access Order

It is important to stress at the outset that an applicant does not have an automatic or absolute right to an Access Order under any circumstances.

Anyone with authority to do required work can apply for an Access Order

The applicant does not have to be the estate owner of the dominant land. As long as the applicant has authority to do the required work he can apply for an Access Order.

It seems that the applicant could be a licensee or one of the statutory undertakers who have power to carry out works on land, but no authority to enter that land for the purpose of carrying out those works.

All interested parties should be served with notice

A very important issue to be clarified at the beginning is "who exactly is going to be named as the respondent". It is possible for a number of different persons to have different interests in one piece of land. There can be any number of respondents. The applicant should try to ensure that he joins, as respondents, anyone who might have a right to prevent him gaining access to the servient land. For example, a person may be a licensee, but not have exclusive possession. If that person is in a position to prevent access he should ideally be approached and if no agreement can be reached he should be joined as a respondent.

As a rule, if the servient land is subject to a mortgage, the applicant does not need to obtain the consent of the mortgagee. It would however be appropriate to add a word of warning here as the Act provides that the terms of an Access Order will be binding on those who subsequently acquire an interest in the servient land, but this does not help against those who have existing rights.

Mortgagees in possession and those taking title from them

What happens if the respondent defaults on his mortgage payments and the mortgagee takes possession and/or subsequently sells the servient land either before or during the access period stated in the Access Order.

The mortgagee is not bound by the Access Order. The applicant having taken the time and trouble (not to mention the cost) of obtaining an Access Order may not be able to enforce it as the mortgagee already had an interest prior to the Access Order. It may be wise to consider the mortgagee as a potential respondent particularly if the works involved are substantial and are going to take some time to complete. If access is only required for a few days the risk will not be so great.

Superior interests in land

This could also apply in a landlord/tenant situation where it might be prudent to liaise with the landlord and if necessary name the landlord as a respondent, in addition to the tenant in occupation. Once the Access Order is made it is binding on anyone acquiring an estate or interest in the land from the respondent.

From the above you will see that it may be necessary to contact a mortgagee or landlord of the servient land. You may not have these details readily to hand and guidance is given in Appendix 8 to help you find this information.

If you need permission to go through several properties in different ownership/occupation you will need to obtain Access Orders against all those owners/occupiers who have not given their consent.

Subsection (1) – Applicant must show failed attempt to obtain access

It is clearly stated in Subsection (1)(b) that a person who needs, but does not have, the consent of some other person to that entry may apply to the court for an Access Order against that other person.

You can therefore only go to court if you need permission and have not managed to obtain it. It follows that in order to make an application for an Access Order it will be necessary to prove that you have tried to obtain consent, but have been unsuccessful. If your attempts to obtain permission fail, only then can you seek an Access Order through the courts. This can prove time consuming and expensive.

Subsection (2) – Applicant must show the works are reasonably necessary

Under Subsection (2)(a) an applicant will need to prove that the works are reasonably necessary for the preservation of the whole or part of the dominant land. The onus is on the applicant to persuade the courts that the works are reasonably necessary. The word "preservation" is vitally important. Only works of maintenance or repair may be carried out under the Act. Actual development, for instance, the building of an extension, is excluded from the provisions of the Act. This is dealt with in greater detail below.

Under Subsection (2)(b) an applicant will also need to satisfy the court that without access the works of preservation cannot be carried out at all, or would be "substantially" more difficult. It is insufficient to show that it is more convenient to have access over the servient land. It must be a necessity.

Subsection (3) – Respondent's right to object

This subsection gives the respondent an opportunity to object to the Access Order on the two grounds stated in Subsection (2)(a) and (2)(b) set out above. The onus is now on the respondent to show that it would be unreasonable for an Access Order to be made.

The applicant can include in his application for an Access Order details of the steps which he is prepared to take to minimise the amount of disturbance to the respondent. For example the applicant could offer to put up temporary screening to maintain some privacy for the respondent whilst the work is being carried out, and state that he will only carry out the work Monday to Friday so that the respondent is not inconvenienced at the weekends. If these suggestions are put forward at the outset they may be viewed favourably by both the respondent and the court.

The court has an overriding discretion to refuse an order on disturbance and hardship grounds. The courts need to find a balance between the nuisance to the respondent if the order is granted and the inconvenience to the applicant if it is not.

Subsection (4) – Basic preservation works

This subsection gives a list, which is not exhaustive, of those works that can be considered to be basic preservation works. The court has discretion to include other works, not specifically mentioned in the Act as basic preservation works. The words "basic preservation works" cannot be repeated often enough as they go to the very heart of the Act, and their importance must not be overlooked. The Act does not restrict the type of basic preservation works for which an Access Order may be sought. However actual development is excluded from the provisions of the Act - only works of maintenance and repair may be carried out. It may not always be easy to prove that the works, which the applicant wishes to carry out, are reasonably necessary to preserve rather than to improve the dominant land.

Subsections (5) and (6) - Improvements or alterations made for their own sake should not be allowed

These subsections broadly follow the recommendations made in paragraphs *4.8 – 4.12 of the Law Commission Report No. 151* which states that improvements or alterations made for their own sake should not be allowed, but those made incidentally to basic preservation should be. In the absence of case law covering this particular issue the Law Commission's recommendations mentioned above have been set out in full in Appendix 3, as this will throw some light on the type of work to be regarded as "incidental" to the basic preservation works. On the other hand, if the work envisaged involves mainly alterations, improvements or demolition, with some small element of basic preservation work included, it is unlikely an Access Order will be granted. There will undoubtedly be disputes over whether some schemes are essentially repairs with incidental improvements or improvements with incidental repairs.

As far as actual demolition is concerned, this work must form part of the general preservation work. Demolition on its own would not warrant the making of an order. It is possible that demolition followed by rebuilding may be permitted but only if the court can be persuaded that these works fall within the term "basic preservation works".

To summarise, the word "incidentally" contained in Subsection (5), makes it clear that if the principal objective is demolition or improvement, with some element of preservation work thrown in, it is unlikely an order will be granted.

Works ancillary to works of preservation, can be included

Works, which are ancillary to the works of preservation, can also be included. For example, it may be permitted to mix concrete on the servient land, if this is the only place that it can be done. However the concrete could only then be used for works covered by the Access Order. Paragraph *4.13 of the Report prepared by the Law Commission* (which is set out in full in Appendix 3) suggested that the right of access should include a right, while the work was being carried out, to place on the servient land materials and equipment needed in the course of the work, as well as anything emanating from the work: for example, rubble from a wall which is demolished. Anyone applying for an Access Order would be well advised to ensure that the Access Order includes all the rights he is likely to need to carry out the works. For example, if the applicant forgets that he needs to bring scaffolding on to the land, and the Access Order does not provide for this, and the applicant is faced with a particularly uncompromising respondent, the applicant may have to go back to court for a second time to get consent for this.

Subsection (7) - Inspections to be classed as works

This subsection provides for inspections to be classed as works which are reasonably necessary for the preservation of the dominant land. If the applicant is faced with a particularly difficult and uncooperative neighbour it appears he may have to apply to the court in the first instance for an order covering inspection, and then depending on what is found, a second application may have to be made to cover entry for the actual works of preservation.

Chapter 6

Section 2: Terms and Conditions of Access Orders

2. (1) An Access Order shall specify-

(a) the works to the dominant land that may be carried out by entering upon the servient land in pursuance of the order;
(b) the particular area of servient land that may be entered upon by virtue of the order for the purpose of carrying out those works to the dominant land; and
(c) the date on which, or the period during which, the land may be so entered upon;

and in the following provisions of this Act any reference to the servient land is a reference to the area specified in the order in pursuance of paragraph (b) above.

(2) An Access Order may impose upon the applicant or the respondent such terms and conditions as appear to the court to be reasonably necessary for the purpose of avoiding or restricting-

(a) any loss, damage, or injury which might otherwise be caused to the respondent or any other person by reason of the entry authorised by the order; or
(b) any inconvenience or loss of privacy that might otherwise be so caused to the respondent or any other person.

(3) Without prejudice to the generality of Subsection (2) above, the terms and conditions which may be imposed under that subsection include provisions with respect to-

(a) the manner in which the specified works are to be carried out;

(b) the days on which, and the hours between which, the work involved may be executed;
(c) the persons who may undertake the carrying out of the specified works or enter upon the servient land under or by virtue of the order;
(d) the taking of any such precautions by the applicant as may be specified in the order.

(4) An Access Order may also impose terms and conditions-

(a) requiring the applicant to pay, or to secure that such person connected with him as may be specified in the order pays, compensation for-

(i) any loss, damage or injury, or
(ii) any substantial loss of privacy or other substantial inconvenience,

which will, or might, be caused to the respondent or any other person by reason of the entry authorised by the order;

(b) requiring the applicant to secure that he, or such person connected with him as may be specified in the order, is insured against any such risks as may be so specified; or
(c) requiring such a record to be made of the condition of the servient land, or of such part of it as may be so specified, as the court may consider expedient with a view to facilitating the determination of any question that may arise concerning damage to that land.

(5) An Access Order may include provision requiring the applicant to pay the respondent such sum by way of consideration for the privilege of entering the servient land in pursuance of the order as appears to the court to be fair and reasonable having regard to all the circumstances of the case, including, in particular-

(a) the likely financial advantage of the order to the applicant and any persons connected with him; and
(b) the degree of inconvenience likely to be caused to the respondent or any other person by the entry;

but no payment shall be ordered under this subsection if and to the extent that the works which the applicant desires to carry out by means of the entry are works to residential land.

(6) For the purposes of Subsection (5)(a) above, the likely financial advantage of an Access Order to the applicant and any persons connected with him shall in all cases be taken to be a sum of money equal to the greater of the following amounts, that is to say-

(a) the amount (if any) by which so much of any likely increase in the value of any land-

(i) which consists of or includes the dominant land, and
(ii) which is owned or occupied by the same person as the dominant land,

as may reasonably be regarded as attributable to the carrying out of the specified works exceeds the likely cost of carrying out those works with the benefit of the Access Order; and

(b) the difference (if it would have been possible to carry out the specified works without entering upon the servient land) between-

(i) the likely cost of carrying out those works without entering upon the servient land; and
(ii) the likely cost of carrying them out with the benefit of the Access Order.

(7) For the purposes of Subsection (5) above, "residential land" means so much of any land as consists of-

(a) a dwelling or part of a dwelling.
(b) a garden, yard, private garage or outbuilding which is used and enjoyed wholly or mainly with a dwelling; or
(c) in the case of a building which includes one or more dwellings, any part of the building which is used and enjoyed wholly or mainly with those dwellings or any of them.

(8) The persons who are to be regarded for the purposes of this section as "connected with" the applicant are-

(a) the owner of any estate or interest in, or right over, the whole or any part of the dominant land;
(b) the occupier of the whole or any part of the dominant land; and
(c) any person whom the applicant may authorise under Section 3(7) below to exercise the power of entry conferred by the Access Order.

(9) The court may make provision-

(a) for the reimbursement by the applicant of any expenses reasonably incurred by the respondent in connection with the application which are not otherwise recoverable as costs;
(b) for the giving of security by the applicant for any sum that might become payable to the respondent or any other person by virtue of this section or Section 3 below.

OBSERVATIONS ON SECTION 2:

This section deals with the terms and conditions of Access Orders which are granted under Section 1 and follows the recommendations set out in paragraph *4.28 of the Law Commission Report* which states that the court should have power to impose conditions on the making of an Access Order with a view to minimising the inconvenience and loss of privacy, the security risks, and the risks of financial loss and physical damage that might be incurred by the respondent or any other person as a result of the order (see Appendix 3).

Subsection (1) – Details required in Access Order

This subsection deals with what shall be specified in an Access Order. It must specify:-

a) the works that can be carried out to the dominant land from the servient land;
b) the particular area of servient land that may be entered for that purpose; and
c) the date on which, or the period during which the servient land may be entered upon.

Great care should be taken in identifying the particular area of the servient land over which access is required. Once the area of servient land is specified it is only this specified area that is covered by the order. Take the following scenario.

The applicant requires access to the respondent's garden so that the applicant can repair the rear wall of his property. The applicant goes to court and obtains an Access Order allowing him access to the respondent's garden. However to get into the respondent's garden he needs to use the alleyway at the side of the respondent's property which is also owned by the respondent. If this alleyway is not specified in the Access Order then the applicant will have no right to use it and he may well have to go back to court for another Access Order.

Subsection (2) – Terms and conditions

Under this subsection the court can impose numerous terms and conditions on both the applicant and the respondent depending upon the individual circumstances of each case. The aim of the court is to provide terms and conditions which are reasonably necessary to prevent or restrict, as much as possible any loss, damage, injury, inconvenience and loss of privacy which might be caused to the respondent, or any other person, as a result of the entry authorised under the Access Order. This subsection makes it clear that an Access Order may permit interference with rights such as restrictive covenants, easements etc.

Subsection (3) – More terms and conditions

This subsection sets out those terms and conditions which may be imposed and include: -

(a) *"the manner in which the specified works are to be carried out"*. The applicant should ensure that he specifies all the works that he could possibly wish to carry out, and the type of plant and equipment which he will need to bring onto the servient land. Those works not specified will not be included in the Access Order and therefore he is not entitled to carry them out under the Access Order.

If works are done which are not permitted by an Access Order the applicant is leaving himself open to an action by the respondent for trespass. Whilst it is unlikely an action for trespass would be brought by a respondent, the very fact that the Act enables a respondent to bring such an action, should act as a deterrent and encourage the applicant to behave himself and only carry out those works authorised by the Access Order.

The Access Order should provide for entry on to the servient land for the purpose of drawing plans and any necessary inspections if it is envisaged that this will be required.

Timescale

(b) *"the days on which, and the hours between which, the work involved may be executed".* When indicating any time scales to the court for completion of the work, the applicant should of course build into these time scales a little leeway to cover poor weather and other unforeseeable difficulties.

Those undertaking the work

(c) *"the persons who may undertake the carrying out of the specified works or enter upon the servient land under or by virtue of the order".* For instance the court could insist that the work is carried out by a reputable tradesman who is to be approved by the respondent. The court is also able to stipulate who may not enter upon the servient land.

Precautions

(d) *"the taking of any such precautions by the applicant as may be specified in the order".* The court could specify that the applicant should take certain precautions to protect the respondent's property. For instance the laying down of ground sheets to catch rubble and chippings and the erection of screening whilst the work is being carried out so that the respondent retains some privacy.

Chapter 6 — Section 2: Terms and Conditions of Access Orders

Subsection (4) - Financial issues

Compensation for any loss, damage, or injury

This subsection begins to deal with the financial issues that can be dealt with in an Access Order. Under this section the court can order the applicant, or such other person connected with him as may be specified in the Access Order to pay to the respondent compensation for any loss, damage, or injury.

At this point I would mention a word of warning to the respondent. As already discussed only those works which are set out in the Access Order are permitted. These permitted works may cause loss to the respondent. If the Access Order makes no mention of compensation to cover such losses it may be difficult for the respondent to obtain compensation for these in the future. It may be possible for an Access Order to include compensation for damage which may be caused. If the applicant and respondent are able to agree to this wording, it would be sensible for the Access Order to provide that the level of compensation can be set by an independent expert without the necessity of going back to court.

Compensation for any substantial loss of privacy or other substantial inconvenience.

This section also states that compensation can be paid for any substantial loss of privacy or other substantial inconvenience. It is possible that damage and loss of privacy are greater at certain times of the year than at others and both the applicant and respondent should have regard to this. Take the example of a respondent who is a retired gentleman who, when the weather is nice, spends hours everyday attending to his beautiful garden. In the spring and summer months his loss is going to be greater, both in respect of loss of privacy and damage to his garden. If the work was carried out during the winter months, his losses would be substantially less. He would not suffer any substantial loss of privacy as he would not be in the garden very much over the winter months, and in the main the plants in his garden would be dormant.

The court may also include in an Access Order a condition that the applicant and/or his contractors be insured against risks specified by the court. Whilst this is at the discretion of the courts, it is more likely than not, that it will be imposed on the applicant, particularly since the application for an Access Order should include details of any existing insurance cover.

Schedule of Condition of servient land prior to access

To help assist in any claims for damages the court can also request that a record of the condition of the servient land, or any specified part of it, be made. In the event of a dispute arising over how much damage has been caused to the servient land, a record of the condition of the servient land, prior to the specified works being commenced will be available.

Subsection (5) – Consideration (as opposed to compensation)

This subsection deals with the payment of consideration rather than compensation. Payment of compensation is discussed above and is payable for loss, damage, injury, substantial loss of privacy, or other substantial inconvenience caused to the respondent and is payable whether or not the dominant land is residential land.

However consideration cannot be ordered to be paid where the dominant land is residential land. Consideration is paid by the applicant to the respondent for the privilege of entering upon the respondent's land. It is in effect a form of wayleave charge. When looking at the amount of consideration to be paid the court will take into account the likely financial advantage of the order to the applicant and the degree of inconvenience to the respondent or any other person.

The applicant can be asked to pay a proportion of the gain which he will make from carrying out the work on the respondent's land and at the inconvenience of the respondent, instead of carrying it out on his own land, at his own inconvenience.

It must be stressed here that consideration is not payable by the applicant if the dominant land is residential land. Residential land is further defined in Subsection (7).

Subsection (6) – Assessment of consideration

This subsection sets out how the likely financial advantage in Subsection (5) is to be calculated. In order to work out the amount of compensation payable under Subsection (5) the court will need to be satisfied that the applicant will obtain a financial advantage (as defined). In a nutshell this is the likely increase in the value of the applicant's land and the difference in the cost of carrying out the works without an Access Order. The applicant should therefore be prepared to put all the relevant figures together and place these before the court. The applicant will need to establish the value of the dominant land in its present state, and its estimated value on completion of the works to be specified in the Access Order. He will also need to produce to the court, two further sets of figures. One in respect of the cost of carrying out the work with the Access Order and another set to cover the likely cost of carrying out the work (where this is possible) without an Access Order.

Subsection (7) - Definition of "residential land"

In this subsection the definition of residential land is very important. As already mentioned, where the applicant seeks to carry out work to residential land no consideration will be payable. Difficult issues will arise especially with mixed user premises such as the shop with flat above. In a case such as this the applicant will no doubt seek to argue that this will fall within the definition of "residential land" as by doing so he will not have to pay the respondent any consideration. On the other hand it will be in the respondent's interest to argue that the applicant's property is a non-residential one, and therefore consideration will be payable.

Subsection (8) – Persons "connected with" the applicant

This subsection sets out those people who are to be regarded as *"connected with"* the applicant during the period of the Access Order. They include the owner of any estate or interest in, or right over the whole or part of the dominant land, the occupier of the whole or any part of the dominant land and includes those persons the applicant reasonably authorises to enter the servient land for the purpose of carrying out the works specified in the Access Order (see Section 3(7)).

Subsection (9) - Court may order the applicant to reimburse the respondent for expenses;
Security for monies due under Sections 2 or 3

This subsection gives the court authority, should it think fit to do so, to order the applicant to reimburse the respondent for any expenses reasonably incurred, where an order for costs is made against the respondent, or if these expenses fall outside the usual order for costs. This might apply in cases where the court has reluctantly ordered costs against a respondent. The court can then redress the balance as it were, by ordering the applicant to pay some of the expenses incurred by the respondent, and so arrive at a financial settlement that is not too harsh on the respondent, who at the end of the day has had to put up with the inconvenience of having the applicant on his land.

Chapter 6 — Section 2: Terms and Conditions of Access Orders

Giving of security by the applicant

Whilst this section sensibly mentions the giving of security by the applicant to cover any sums that may become due to the respondent, it unfortunately does not go on to state when such security should be paid, to whom, or how such sum should be calculated.

Chapter 7

Section 3: Effect of Access Order

(1) An Access Order requires the respondent, so far as he has power to do so, to permit the applicant or any of his associates to do anything which the applicant or associate is authorised or required to do under or by virtue of the order or this section.

(2) Except as otherwise provided by or under this Act, an Access Order authorises the applicant or any of his associates, without the consent of the respondent, -

(a) to enter upon the servient land for the purpose of carrying out the specified works;
(b) to bring on to that land, leave there during the period permitted by the order and, before the end of that period, remove, such materials, plant and equipment as are reasonably necessary for the carrying out of those works; and
(c) to bring on to that land any waste arising from the carrying out of those works, if it is reasonably necessary to do so in the course of removing it from the dominant land;

but nothing in this Act or in any Access Order shall authorise the applicant or any of his associates to leave anything in, on or over the servient land (otherwise than in discharge of their duty to make good that land) after their entry for the purpose of carrying out works to the dominant land ceases to be authorised under or by virtue of the order.

(3) An Access Order requires the applicant-

(a) to secure that any waste arising from the carrying out of the specified works is removed from the servient land forthwith;

(b) to secure that, before the entry ceases to be authorised under or by virtue of the order, the servient land is, so far as reasonably practicable, made good; and

(c) to indemnify the respondent against any damage which may be caused to the servient land or any goods by the applicant or any of his associates which would not have been so caused had the order not been made;

but this subsection is subject to Subsections (4) and (5) below.

(4) In making an Access Order, the court may vary or exclude, in whole or in part,-

(a) any authorisation that would otherwise be conferred by Subsection (2)(b) or (c) above; or

(b) any requirement that would otherwise be imposed by Subsection (3) above.

(5) Without prejudice to the generality of Subsection (4) above, if the court is satisfied that it is reasonably necessary for any such waste as may arise from the carrying out of the specified works to be left on the servient land for some period before removal, the Access Order may, in place of Subsection (3)(a) above, include provision-

(a) authorising the waste to be left on that land for such period as may be permitted by the order; and

(b) requiring the applicant to secure that the waste is removed before the end of that period.

(6) Where the applicant or any of his associates is authorised or required under or by virtue of an Access Order or this section to enter, or do any other thing, upon the servient land, he shall not (as respects that Access Order) be taken to be a trespasser from the beginning on account of his, or any other person's, subsequent conduct.

(7) For the purposes of this section, the applicant's "associates" are such number of persons (whether or not servants or agents of his) whom he may reasonably authorise under this subsection to exercise the power of entry conferred by the Access Order as may be reasonably necessary for carrying out the specified works.

OBSERVATIONS ON SECTION 3:

General

The provisions of this particular section interact with one another in a sometimes confusing and complex way and at times appear to be contradictory. Great care will need to be taken in the completion of the applicant's application for an Access Order and the respondent's reply.

Subsection (1) – Permits the applicant to do anything authorised either by the Act or the Access Order

Under this subsection the effect of an Access Order is to require the respondent, so far as he has power to do so, to permit the applicant and his associates to do anything authorised either by the Act itself or the Access Order and is based on the recommendation contained in *paragraph 4.106 of the Law Commission Report* (see Appendix 3). The respondent must allow the applicant and/or his associates to enter the servient land for the purpose of the access specified in the Access Order and for the purpose of enjoying those rights that may be attached to the Access Order.

Damages for breach of the terms or conditions

If, after being granted an Access Order, an applicant is faced with a difficult and obstructive respondent who refuses to allow the access stipulated in the Access Order, the applicant may make an application for damages for breach of the terms or conditions of the Access Order.

Although the Act does not specify how the application should be made, it is thought that the application should be brought within the original proceedings which led to the Access Order being granted *(use Court Form N244 and state that the application is brought under Section 6(2) of the Access to Neighbouring Land Act 1992).*

Subsection (2) - right of access, if granted by the court, should extend to anyone reasonably assisting the applicant and for anything emanating from the work

This subsection is based on the recommendation made in *paragraph 4.13 of the Law Commission Report* which stated that the right of access, if granted by the court, should extend to anyone reasonably assisting the applicant (See Appendix 3). This is to enable the applicant's contractors, and others who may be assisting the applicant, to enter upon the servient land. It also goes on to recommend that a right of access should include a right, whilst the work is being carried on, to place on the respondent's land any materials and equipment needed in the course of the work, as well as anything emanating from the work, and gives as two examples, rubble from a wall which is being demolished and branches from a tree.

Respondent should list any matters which could give rise to a dispute

Respondents to an application will need to pay particular attention to this subsection. The words at the very beginning of this subsection *"Except as otherwise provided by or under this Act"* implies certain terms into an Access Order unless the Access Order or the Act says otherwise. This subsection can be construed so widely that the respondent should seek in his reply to the applicant's application to ensure that any matters which could give rise to a dispute between the applicant and the respondent are clearly defined so that they can be set out in the Access Order. In certain circumstances the respondent may wish to restrict exactly what can be brought on to his land and he should ensure this is specified in the Access Order.

Respondent should ensure that the order required that nothing foreign is left on his land

Another point of importance is that nothing can be left in, on or over the servient land once the entry authorised by the Access Order has come to an end. This means that pipes, wires, cables, conduits, props, supports, foundations, footings, or anything else you can conceivably think of, cannot be left in on or over the servient land. Where this is essential to the work which the applicant wishes to carry out, the applicant will need to obtain the respondent's Agreement to this as an entirely separate issue, as this is not something which the respondent can be ordered to comply with under this Act. It should be noted that the removal of waste from the servient land can be relaxed somewhat by Subsection (5) which gives the court the opportunity to allow the applicant to leave waste on the servient land for the period specified in the Access Order.

Subsection (3) - The servient land should, as far as is reasonably practicable, be fully reinstated

This is based on the recommendations contained in *paragraphs 4.30, 4.31 and 4.50 of the Law Commission Report* which sensibly states that the property entered (the servient land) should, as far as is reasonably practicable, be fully reinstated and any damage made good (see Appendix 3).

The terms which can be imposed on the applicant are defined in this section. However when making an Access Order the court is able to vary or exclude all of these provisions apart from the right of entry given to the applicant by Subsection (2)(a).

An Access Order will normally require the applicant to remove waste from the servient land before expiry of the authorised period set out in the Access Order, unless there is a provision to the contrary in the order.

The applicant must make good any damage as far as possible and leave the servient land in the same condition in which he found it. Provided a Report/Schedule of Condition was prepared on the servient land prior to the works being carried out by the applicant, there should be no difficulties here. When dealing with the time limits to be specified in the Access Order the applicant should ensure that he will have sufficient time to carry out the work on his own property and to reinstate the servient land. Alternatively, and whilst the Act does not specifically provide for this, it could be that the applicant and respondent may prefer for a payment of money to pass from the applicant to the respondent in lieu of the applicant making good. As long as this is agreed between the parties it should be perfectly acceptable as an alternative.

This subsection may be varied or excluded under Subsections (4) and (5).

Subsection (4) - Variations and exclusions

This subsection makes it clear that all the terms implied into an Access Order by Subsections (2) and (3) can be varied or excluded, except the right of entry given by Subsection (2) (a).

Subsection (5) - Variations and exclusions

This subsection provides that Subsections (3)(a) and (4) can be varied with regard to any waste to be left on the servient land.

Subsection (6) - Entry under Access Order deemed to be with the respondent's consent

The reasoning behind this subsection is to avoid the instigation of the rule stated in the *Six Carpenters Case (1610)* which is mentioned in *paragraph 4.111 of the Law Commission Report* (see Appendix 3). The effect of this rule is that *"where a person enters land with lawful authority, and subsequently abuses that authority, he becomes a trespasser ab initio, and his misconduct relates back so as to make his original entry tortious".* It is however most unlikely that this rule could apply to entry pursuant to an Access Order as the rule would only apply where the applicant enters land under an authority given by law, whereas entry under an Access Order is deemed to be with the respondent's consent. It appears this subsection has been included so that there is no doubt as to the position.

Subsection (7) - Defines the applicant's associates

This subsection defines the applicant's associates. Associates may widely be defined as anyone the applicant may reasonably authorise to carry out the work specified in the Access Order. The respondent might quite rightly be concerned about this. At the end of the day he should remain, to a degree, *"the king of his castle"* and should not be expected to allow all and sundry on to his property. If the applicant's past behaviour (or the behaviour of anyone likely to be treated as an associate) has caused difficulties for the respondent, the respondent should make this known to the court and indicate that whilst he has no objection to an Access Order (if that be the case) he would like the Access Order to specify exactly who is to be regarded as authorised to enter the servient land and who is to carry out the work specified in the Access Order. Take the following scenario which is not untypical of the type of case likely to come before the court:-

The applicant is a keen DIY enthusiast who has already been given access to the respondent's garden to repoint his boundary wall. This initial access was given by neighbourly consent in the usual way.

However on that occasion the applicant stepped all over the respondent's flower beds, dumped his rubble on top of his neighbour's compost heap, and left chippings on the grass which subsequently damaged the respondent's lawnmower. To add further insult to injury when the applicant carried out the re-pointing to his boundary wall he had forgotten to dampen the walls, and the mortar subsequently came away from the wall and fell onto the respondent's flowerbeds causing further damage.

The respondent mentioned these problems to the applicant who then asked for permission to go back and have another try at repointing his boundary wall. The respondent not surprisingly was rather reluctant to allow this and suggested that a qualified builder should carry out the work. The applicant took this as an insult to his DIY skills and refused to ask a builder to carry out the work. Neighbourly relations then went downhill fast. If the applicant were to apply for an Access Order to enable him to have another go at repointing his boundary wall, the respondent would be perfectly entitled to request the court to specify that the work should only be carried out by a suitably qualified builder to avoid any further problems.

As the scenario set out above is so typical of the way in which arguments between neighbours can escalate and get out of hand, I have based some of the precedents in Appendix 9 on this scenario.

Chapter 8

Section 4: Persons bound by Access Order, unidentified persons and bar on contracting out

4. (1) In addition to the respondent, an Access Order shall, subject to the provisions of the Land Charges Act 1972 and the Land Registration Act 1925, be binding on-

(a) any of his successors in title to the servient land; and
(b) any person who has an estate or interest in, or right over, the whole or any part of the servient land which was created after the making of the order and who derives his title to that estate, interest or right under the respondent;

and references to the respondent shall be construed accordingly.

(2) If and to the extent that the court considers it just and equitable to allow him to do so, a person on whom an Access Order becomes binding by virtue of Subsection (1)(a) or (b) above shall be entitled, as respects anything falling to be done after the order becomes binding on him, to enforce the order or any of its terms or conditions as if he were the respondent, and references to the respondent shall be construed accordingly.

(3) Rules of court may-

(a) provide a procedure which may be followed where the applicant does not know, and cannot reasonably ascertain, the name of any person whom he desires to make respondent to the application; and

(b) make provision enabling such an applicant to make such a person respondent by description instead of by name;

and in this subsection "applicant" includes a person who proposes to make an application for an Access Order.

(4) Any agreement, whenever made, shall be void if and to the extent that it would, apart from this subsection, prevent a person from applying for an Access Order or restrict his right to do so.

OBSERVATIONS ON SECTION 4:

Miscellaneous provisions and contracting out prohibited

This section sets out some miscellaneous provisions. It covers the making of Access Orders binding on successors in title of the servient land. It is not however clear anywhere in the Act whether the Access Order is available to the successors in title of the dominant land. It enables persons who were not a party to the Access Order to enforce the terms of the Access Order in limited circumstances and allows for rules of court to be made in circumstances where the respondent is unknown, and finally it prohibits contracting out of the Act.

It should be noted that whilst the Access Order itself does not confer an interest in land it does create a right which, to an extent runs to bind successors in title of that land, and so has some of the characteristics of an interest in land.

Subsection (1) – Who will be bound by an Access Order

This subsection sets out who will be bound by the Access Order once it has been made. There is of course the respondent which should not pose any great problem, as he would have been identified in the Access Order. Subsection (1) (a) mentions the successors in title to the servient land. The extent to which successors in title are bound depends upon registration of the Access Order which is dealt with in more detail in the next section.

Under Subsection (1) (b) an Access Order can be binding on licensees, lessees and underlessees. In a nutshell anyone who derives his title to the servient land, or acquires any interest or right in the servient land via the respondent can be bound by the Access Order.

Subsection (2) – Successors in title to servient tenement

This subsection serves to remind us that the respondent and his successors in title do have some rights under the Act. The court has (to the extent that it considers just and equitable) a discretion to enforce the Access Order and its terms and conditions in favour of the respondent's successors in title. This particular clause could come into play in the following circumstances. The applicant, who owns a commercial property, has gone off to court and got his Access Order. In the meantime the respondent sells the servient land before the work authorised by the Access Order has been started. The Access Order now becomes binding on the new owners of the servient land who step into the shoes of the original respondent.

These new respondents could now claim, should they wish to do so, any financial compensation and consideration, which can be payable when the dominant land is a commercial property (see Sections 4, 5 and 6). Likewise the Access Order, in all probability, will have a condition attached to it stating that before the entry authorised by the order takes place, the applicant should have the appropriate insurance.

If the applicant subsequently refuses to take out this insurance, the new respondents can seek to have this condition enforced. As will be seen this subsection unfortunately contains a proviso to the effect that the court will only enforce such conditions if it considers it just and equitable to do so. This proviso itself is totally unjust. The new respondents are merely seeking to have enforced a condition which is already included in the Access Order. Why should they now have to convince the court that it is just and equitable to enforce this original condition? This is another erosion of respondents' rights as landowners.

Subsection (3) – On whom should notice requiring access, be served?

This subsection enables rules of court to be made to cover the situation where the applicant has been unable to ascertain who owns the servient land. The procedure for making an application for an Access Order is contained in Order 49 Rule 1 of the County Court Supplementary Rules as amended which is set out in full in Appendix 4.

These rules state the information to be included in an application for an Access Order and are fairly straightforward.

However Rule 1(4) states that the respondent shall be the owner and the occupier of the servient land, whereas the Act states that you obtain an Access Order against the person whose permission you need to gain entry to enable you to do the work. It must be stressed again that care will need to be taken when deciding who to name as the respondent. If an applicant just names as a respondent the person who controls entry to the servient land as required by the Act, and that person is not the owner/occupier, the applicant runs the risk of being unsuccessful as he has not complied with the rules which state that the respondent shall be the owner and the occupier of the servient land. As will be seen the rules appear to contradict the Act and I do not think there are any easy answers to deal with this particular problem.

Subsection (4) – Contracting out forbidden

The effect of this subsection is to render void any attempt to prevent a person from applying for an Access Order or to restrict that person's right to apply for an Access Order. It forbids agreements contracting out of the Act and applies to any agreement made before or after the Act. Despite this, from the respondent's point of view, it may be worth including in an Agreement a clause restricting the applicant's right to an Access Order.

Whilst the actual clause will be void, it may be taken into account when considering the level of interference or disturbance which the respondent could be expected to suffer if the Access Order was granted. If the respondent did not think the access would interfere with the enjoyment of his land, he would not have inserted the clause. Likewise if the applicant did not think he could manage without the access he would not have agreed to it and must have thought that he could manage without entry on to the respondent's property.

Chapter 9

Section 5: Registration of Access Orders and of applications for such orders

5. (1) In Section 6(1) of the Land Charges Act 1972 (which specifies the writs and orders affecting land that may be entered in the register) after paragraph (c) there shall be added-

"(d) any Access Order under the Access to Neighbouring Land Act 1992."

(2) In Section 49 of the Land Registration Act 1925 (rules to provide for certain rights, interests and claims to be protected by notice) in Subsection (1) (which specifies those rights, interests and claims) after paragraph (h) there shall be added-

"(j) Access Orders under the Access to Neighbouring Land Act 1992 which, notwithstanding Section 59 of this Act, it may be deemed expedient to protect by notice instead of by caution."

(3) In Section 64 of that Act (production of certificates for noting on certain dealings etc.) after Subsection (6) there shall be added-

"(7) Subsection (1) above shall also not require the production of the land certificate or of any charge certificate when a person applies for the registration of a notice in respect of an Access Order under the Access to Neighbouring Land Act 1992."

(4) In any case where-

(a) an Access Order is discharged under Section 6(1)(a) below; and

(b) the order has been protected by an entry registered under the Land Charges Act 1972 or by a notice or caution under the Land Registration Act 1925,

the court may by order direct that the entry, notice or caution shall be cancelled.

(5) The rights conferred on a person by or under an Access Order are not capable of constituting an overriding interest within the meaning of the Land Registration Act 1925, notwithstanding that he or any other person is in actual occupation of the whole or any part of the servient land in question.

(6) An application for an Access Order shall be regarded as a pending land action for the purposes of the Land Charges Act 1972 and the Land Registration Act 1925.

OBSERVATIONS ON SECTION 5:

Registration of Access Orders

Access Orders can be registered under the Land Charges Act 1972 and the Land Registration Act 1925. This particular section of the Act contains important notes on the procedure to be followed and deals with both registered and unregistered land.

Subsection (1) - Applicant's responsibility if he wishes to register

As a result of this Act Section 6(1) of the Land Charges Act 1972 was amended by the addition of an extra clause which enabled an Access Order in respect of unregistered land to be registered as a writ or order. It is the applicant's responsibility to attend to the Registration. The court will not do this. The Registration is effected by preparing a Land Charge Form K4 and submitting this to the Land Charges Registry.

Subsection (2) – Registration where servient land has a registered title

This subsection deals with the position should the servient land be registered land. That is to say it is registered with a title number at the Land Registry. It provides for Access Orders to be registered at the Land Registry by a notice rather than a caution. It seems that the applicant could opt to register a caution rather than a notice. The applicant should be very wary of registering a caution when a notice will do. If the respondent as a result of a wrongly registered caution suffers loss (for example, the respondent could have a buyer for the servient land, who will not complete that purchase until the caution has been removed, which will take time) there is a strong possibility that the applicant could be held responsible for those losses.

Subsection (3) - Land Certificate not required for registration

This subsection enables the applicant to register the Access Order at the Land Registry without production of the respondent's Land or Charge Certificate. This is just as well, as it is highly unlikely that a respondent would willingly hand over his Land Certificate to the applicant, or in the alternative be prepared to place his Land Certificate on deposit at the Land Registry. If there is a mortgage on the servient land then there will of course be a Charge Certificate instead of a Land Certificate which will usually be held by the respondent's mortgage provider as security. However during the last couple of years it has become increasingly popular for mortgage providers to request the Land Registry to retain Charge Certificates under Section 63 of the Land Registration Act 1925.

Subsection (4) - any party to the Access Order can apply for it to be discharged

This subsection states that under Subsection 6(1)(a) below any party to the Access Order can apply for it to be discharged. When making such an application it should include a request specifically asking the court to direct that the relevant Land Charge entry (writ or order) (for unregistered land) or Land Registry notice (for registered land) should be cancelled. If a specific request for this is not made, the court will not include this in the order. In the absence of a direction from the court it is only the person who registered the relevant entry who can remove it, namely the applicant. To cancel a Land Charge Entry use Land Charge Form K11.

Subsection (5) – Overriding interest not acquired

In cases where the servient land is registered land, this subsection prevents a person who has the advantage of an Access Order from acquiring an overriding interest in the servient land.

Subsection (6) - Application, for an Access Order can be registered as a pending land action at the Land Charges Registry or the Land Registry

Subsection (6) states that an application, and I repeat the word application, for an Access Order can be registered as a Pending Land Action at the Land Charges Registry or the Land Registry depending upon whether or not the servient land is unregistered or registered. In the case of unregistered land a Pending Land Action will not bind a purchaser of the servient land without express notice unless it is registered at the Land Charges Registry using Land Charge Form K3. In the case of registered land, a Pending Land Action is registered as a caution. Should an applicant decide to register a caution, Land Registry Form CT2 should be used. To withdraw the caution use Land Registry Form WCT. I would suggest that if an applicant has registered a caution he should keep form WCT in a prominent position in his file, so that he does not forget to apply to the Land Registry to have the caution removed once it is no longer required.

Once the Access Order has been obtained the Pending Land Action should be cancelled and replaced by the registration of a writ or order/notice in accordance with Subsections (1) and (2) above.

Chapter 10

Section 6: Variation of orders and damages for breach

6. (1) Where an Access Order or an order under this subsection has been made, the court may, on the application of any party to the proceedings in which the order was made or of any other person on whom the order is binding-

(a) discharge or vary the order or any of its terms or conditions;
(b) suspend any of its terms or conditions; or
(c) revive any term or condition suspended under paragraph (b) above;

and in the application of Subsections (1) and (2) of Section 4 above in relation to an Access Order, any order under this subsection which relates to the Access Order shall be treated for the purposes of those subsections as included in the Access Order.

(2) If any person contravenes or fails to comply with any requirement, term or condition imposed upon him by or under this Act, the court may, without prejudice to any other remedy available, make an order for the payment of damages by him to any other person affected by the contravention or failure who makes an application for relief under this subsection.

OBSERVATIONS ON SECTION 6:

Subsection (1) - Application for discharge, variation, suspension or reinstatement of Access Order

This subsection allows any party bound by an Access Order to apply to the court for it to be discharged, varied, suspended or reinstated. A precedent for the Variation of an Access Order can be found in Appendix 9. Neither the Act nor the rules of court give any time limit within which the application is to be made. This subsection follows paragraphs *4.74 – 4.76 of the Law Commission Report,* details of which are set out in Appendix 3.

Subsection (2) - Damages

This subsection creates a remedy of damages in the event that a party to the Access Order fails to comply with it. However the Act is silent as to exactly how damages are to be calculated. It should be noted that the Act states that *"any other person affected by the contravention or failure ..."* may make a claim for damages. It is not necessary for that other person to have been a party to the Access Order. All he has to do is prove that he has suffered a loss as a result of the breach. A precedent for a claim for damages can be found in Appendix 9.

Chapter 11

Section 7: Jurisdiction over and allocation of proceedings

7. (1) The High Court and the County Courts shall both have jurisdiction under this Act.

(2) In article 4 of the High Court and County Courts Jurisdiction Order 1991 (which provides that proceedings in which the County Courts and the High Court both have jurisdiction may, subject to articles 5 and 6, be commenced either in a County Court or in the High Court) for the words "and 6" there shall be substituted the words", 6 and 6A"; and after article 6 of that order there shall be inserted-

"6A. Applications under Section 1 of the Access to Neighbouring Land Act 1992 shall be commenced in a County Court."

(3) The amendment by Subsection (2) above of provisions contained in an order shall not be taken to have prejudiced any power to make further orders revoking or amending those provisions.

OBSERVATIONS ON SECTION 7:

Jurisdiction of the courts

This section gives both the High Court and County Court jurisdiction and gives effect to paragraphs *4.88-4.93 of the Law Commission Report* (set out in full in Appendix 3). The County Court will have initial jurisdiction in any proceedings brought under this Act. It is possible for proceedings to be transferred to the High Court but this is likely to happen only in rare circumstances.

Chapter 12

Section 8: Interpretation and application

8. (1) Any reference in this Act to an "entry" upon any servient land includes a reference to the doing on that land of anything necessary for carrying out the works to the dominant land which are reasonably necessary for its preservation; and "enter" shall be construed accordingly.

(2) This Act applies in relation to any obstruction of, or other interference with, a right over, or interest in, any land as it applies in relation to an entry upon that land; and "enter" and "entry" shall be constructed accordingly.

(3) In this Act-

"Access Order" has the meaning given by Section 1(1) above;

"applicant" means a person making an application for an Access Order and, subject to Section 4 above, "the respondent" means the respondent, or any of the respondents, to such an application;

"the court" means the High Court or a County Court;

"the dominant land" and "the servient land" respectively have the meanings given by Section 1(1) above, but subject, in the case of servient land, to Section 2(1) above;

"land" does not include a highway;

"the specified works" means the works specified in the Access Order in pursuance of Section 2(1)(a) above.

OBSERVATIONS ON SECTION 8:

Subsection (1) – Catch all contingency clause to allow work to proceed even if Access Order overlooks something

Attention needs to be paid to this subsection which appears to have been written into the Act in case anything has been overlooked in the preparation of the Access Order. It allows work to be carried on to the dominant land even if these works are not specified in the Access Order. This contradicts Subsection (2)(1) which clearly states that the Access Order *"shall specify the works to the dominant land that may be carried out"*.

Subsection (2) - Easements and rights of way

This subsection makes it clear that an Access Order will allow the applicant to interfere with rights of way, easements etc. during the period specified in the Access Order.

Subsection (3) - Definitions

This subsection of the Act also includes some definitions. Further definitions can be found in Appendix 5.

Chapter 13

Short Title, Commencement and Extent

Section 9

9. (1) This Act may be cited as the Access to Neighbouring Land Act 1992.

(2) This Act shall come into force on such day as the Lord Chancellor may by order made by statutory instrument appoint.

(3) This Act extends to England and Wales only.

OBSERVATIONS ON SECTION 9:

This section gives the title of the Act and states that it shall come into force when the Lord Chancellor makes an order to that effect.

Date Act came into force

The Act came into force on the 31st January 1993.

Appendix 1

Access to Neighbouring Land Act 1992

An Act to enable persons who desire to carry out works to any land which are reasonably necessary for the preservation of that land to obtain access to neighbouring land in order to do so; and for purposes connected therewith.
[16th March 1992]

Be it enacted by the Queen's most Excellent Majesty, by and with the advice and consent of the Lords Spiritual and Temporal, and Commons, in this present Parliament assembled, and by the authority of the same, as follows:—

Access Orders.

1. (1) A person—

(a) who, for the purpose of carrying out works to any land (the "dominant land"), desires to enter upon any adjoining or adjacent land (the "servient land"), and
(b) who needs, but does not have, the consent of some other person to that entry,

may make an application to the court for an order under this section ("an Access Order") against that other person.

(2) On an application under this section, the court shall make an Access Order if, and only if, it is satisfied—

(a) that the works are reasonably necessary for the preservation of the whole or any part of the dominant land; and

(b) that they cannot be carried out, or would be substantially more difficult to carry out, without entry upon the servient land;

but this subsection is subject to Subsection (3) below.

(3) The court shall not make an Access Order in any case where it is satisfied that, were it to make such an order—

(a) the respondent or any other person would suffer interference with, or disturbance of, his use or enjoyment of the servient land, or
(b) the respondent, or any other person (whether of full age or capacity or not) in occupation of the whole or any part of the servient land, would suffer hardship,

to such a degree by reason of the entry (notwithstanding any requirement of this Act or any term or condition that may be imposed under it) that it would be unreasonable to make the order.

(4) Where the court is satisfied on an application under this section that it is reasonably necessary to carry out any basic preservation works to the dominant land, those works shall be taken for the purposes of this Act to be reasonably necessary for the preservation of the land; and in this subsection "basic preservation works" means any of the following, that is to say—

(a) the maintenance, repair or renewal of any part of a building or other structure comprised in, or situate on, the dominant land;
(b) the clearance, repair or renewal of any drain, sewer, pipe or cable so comprised or situate;
(c) the treatment, cutting back, felling, removal or replacement of any hedge, tree, shrub or other growing thing which is

so comprised and which is, or is in danger of becoming, damaged, diseased, dangerous, insecurely rooted or dead;

(d) the filling in, or clearance, of any ditch so comprised;

but this subsection is without prejudice to the generality of the works which may, apart from it, be regarded by the court as reasonably necessary for the preservation of any land.

(5) If the court considers it fair and reasonable in all the circumstances of the case, works may be regarded for the purposes of this Act as being reasonably necessary for the preservation of any land (or, for the purposes of Subsection (4) above, as being basic preservation works which it is reasonably necessary to carry out to any land) notwithstanding that the works incidentally involve—

(a) the making of some alteration, adjustment or improvement to the land, or

(b) the demolition of the whole or any part of a building or structure comprised in or situate upon the land.

(6) Where any works are reasonably necessary for the preservation of the whole or any part of the dominant land, the doing to the dominant land of anything which is requisite for, incidental to, or consequential on, the carrying out of those works shall be treated for the purposes of this Act as the carrying out of works which are reasonably necessary for the preservation of that land; and references in this Act to works, or to the carrying out of works, shall be construed accordingly.

(7) Without prejudice to the generality of Subsection (6) above, if it is reasonably necessary for a person to inspect the dominant land—

(a) for the purpose of ascertaining whether any works may be reasonably necessary for the preservation of the whole or any part of that land,
(b) for the purpose of making any map or plan, or ascertaining the course of any drain, sewer, pipe or cable, in preparation for, or otherwise in connection with, the carrying out of works which are so reasonably necessary, or
(c) otherwise in connection with the carrying out of any such works,

the making of such an inspection shall be taken for the purposes of this Act to be the carrying out to the dominant land of works which are reasonably necessary for the preservation of that land; and references in this Act to works, or to the carrying out of works, shall be construed accordingly.

Terms and conditions of Access Orders.

2. (1) An Access Order shall specify—

(a) the works to the dominant land that may be carried out by entering upon the servient land in pursuance of the order;
(b) the particular area of servient land that may be entered upon by virtue of the order for the purpose of carrying out those works to the dominant land; and
(c) the date on which, or the period during which, the land may be so entered upon;

and in the following provisions of this Act any reference to the servient land is a reference to the area specified in the order in pursuance of paragraph (b) above.

(2) An Access Order may impose upon the applicant or the respondent such terms and conditions as appear to the court to

be reasonably necessary for the purpose of avoiding or restricting—

(a) any loss, damage, or injury which might otherwise be caused to the respondent or any other person by reason of the entry authorised by the order; or
(b) any inconvenience or loss of privacy that might otherwise be so caused to the respondent or any other person.

(3) Without prejudice to the generality of Subsection (2) above, the terms and conditions which may be imposed under that subsection include provisions with respect to—
(a) the manner in which the specified works are to be carried out;
(b) the days on which, and the hours between which, the work involved may be executed;
(c) the persons who may undertake the carrying out of the specified works or enter upon the servient land under or by virtue of the order;
(d) the taking of any such precautions by the applicant as may be specified in the order.

(4) An Access Order may also impose terms and conditions—

(a) requiring the applicant to pay, or to secure that such person connected with him as may be specified in the order pays, compensation for—

(i) any loss, damage or injury, or
(ii) any substantial loss of privacy or other substantial inconvenience,

which will, or might, be caused to the respondent or any other person by reason of the entry authorised by the order;

(b) requiring the applicant to secure that he, or such person connected with him as may be specified in the order, is insured against any such risks as may be so specified; or
(c) requiring such a record to be made of the condition of the servient land, or of such part of it as may be so specified, as the court may consider expedient with a view to facilitating the determination of any question that may arise concerning damage to that land.

(5) An Access Order may include provision requiring the applicant to pay the respondent such sum by way of consideration for the privilege of entering the servient land in pursuance of the order as appears to the court to be fair and reasonable having regard to all the circumstances of the case, including, in particular—

(a) the likely financial advantage of the order to the applicant and any persons connected with him; and
(b) the degree of inconvenience likely to be caused to the respondent or any other person by the entry;

but no payment shall be ordered under this subsection if and to the extent that the works which the applicant desires to carry out by means of the entry are works to residential land.

(6) For the purposes of Subsection (5)(a) above, the likely financial advantage of an Access Order to the applicant and any persons connected with him shall in all cases be taken to be a sum of money equal to the greater of the following amounts, that is to say—

(a) the amount (if any) by which so much of any likely increase in the value of any land—

(i) which consists of or includes the dominant land, and

(ii) which is owned or occupied by the same person as the dominant land,

as may reasonably be regarded as attributable to the carrying out of the specified works exceeds the likely cost of carrying out those works with the benefit of the Access Order; and

(b) the difference (if it would have been possible to carry out the specified works without entering upon the servient land) between—

(i) the likely cost of carrying out those works without entering upon the servient land; and

(ii) the likely cost of carrying them out with the benefit of the Access Order.

(7) For the purposes of Subsection (5) above, "residential land" means so much of any land as consists of—

(a) a dwelling or part of a dwelling;
(b) a garden, yard, private garage or outbuilding which is used and enjoyed wholly or mainly with a dwelling; or
(c) in the case of a building which includes one or more dwellings, any part of the building which is used and enjoyed wholly or mainly with those dwellings or any of them.

(8) The persons who are to be regarded for the purposes of this section as "connected with" the applicant are—

(a) the owner of any estate or interest in, or right over, the whole or any part of the dominant land;

(b) the occupier of the whole or any part of the dominant land; and

(c) any person whom the applicant may authorise under Section 3(7) below to exercise the power of entry conferred by the Access Order.

(9) The court may make provision—

(a) for the reimbursement by the applicant of any expenses reasonably incurred by the respondent in connection with the application which are not otherwise recoverable as costs;

(b) for the giving of security by the applicant for any sum that might become payable to the respondent or any other person by virtue of this section or Section 3 below.

Effect of Access Order.

3. (1) An Access Order requires the respondent, so far as he has power to do so, to permit the applicant or any of his associates to do anything which the applicant or associate is authorised or required to do under or by virtue of the order or this section.

(2) Except as otherwise provided by or under this Act, an Access Order authorises the applicant or any of his associates, without the consent of the respondent,—

(a) to enter upon the servient land for the purpose of carrying out the specified works;

(b) to bring on to that land, leave there during the period permitted by the order and, before the end of that period, remove, such materials, plant and equipment as are reasonably necessary for the carrying out of those works; and

(c) to bring on to that land any waste arising from the carrying out of those works, if it is reasonably necessary to do so in the course of removing it from the dominant land;

but nothing in this Act or in any Access Order shall authorise the applicant or any of his associates to leave anything in, on or over the servient land (otherwise than in discharge of their duty to make good that land) after their entry for the purpose of carrying out works to the dominant land ceases to be authorised under or by virtue of the order.

(3) An Access Order requires the applicant—

(a) to secure that any waste arising from the carrying out of the specified works is removed from the servient land forthwith;
(b) to secure that, before the entry ceases to be authorised under or by virtue of the order, the servient land is, so far as reasonably practicable, made good; and
(c) to indemnify the respondent against any damage which may be caused to the servient land or any goods by the applicant or any of his associates which would not have been so caused had the order not been made;

but this subsection is subject to Subsections (4) and (5) below.

(4) In making an Access Order, the court may vary or exclude, in whole or in part,—

(a) any authorisation that would otherwise be conferred by Subsection (2)(b) or (c) above; or
(b) any requirement that would otherwise be imposed by Subsection (3) above.

(5) Without prejudice to the generality of Subsection (4) above, if the court is satisfied that it is reasonably necessary for any such waste as may arise from the carrying out of the specified works to be left on the servient land for some period before removal, the Access Order may, in place of Subsection (3)(a) above, include provision—

(a) authorising the waste to be left on that land for such period as may be permitted by the order; and

(b) requiring the applicant to secure that the waste is removed before the end of that period.

(6) Where the applicant or any of his associates is authorised or required under or by virtue of an Access Order or this section to enter, or do any other thing, upon the servient land , he shall not (as respects that Access Order) be taken to be a trespasser from the beginning on account of his, or any other person's, subsequent conduct.

(7) For the purposes of this section, the applicant's “associates” are such number of persons (whether or not servants or agents of his) whom he may reasonably authorise under this subsection to exercise the power of entry conferred by the Access Order as may be reasonably necessary for carrying out the specified works.

Persons bound by Access Order, unidentified persons and bar on contracting out.

4. (1) In addition to the respondent, an Access Order shall, subject to the provisions of the [1972 c. 61] Land Charges Act 1972 and the [1925 c. 21] Land Registration Act 1925, be binding on—

(a) any of his successors in title to the servient land; and

(b) any person who has an estate or interest in, or right over, the whole or any part of the servient land which was created after the making of the order and who derives his title to that estate, interest or right under the respondent;

and references to the respondent shall be construed accordingly.

(2) If and to the extent that the court considers it just and equitable to allow him to do so, a person on whom an Access Order becomes binding by virtue of Subsection (1)(a) or (b) above shall be entitled, as respects anything falling to be done after the order becomes binding on him, to enforce the order or any of its terms or conditions as if he were the respondent, and references to the respondent shall be construed accordingly.

(3) Rules of court may—

(a) provide a procedure which may be followed where the applicant does not know, and cannot reasonably ascertain, the name of any person whom he desires to make respondent to the application; and
(b) make provision enabling such an applicant to make such a person respondent by description instead of by name;

and in this subsection "applicant" includes a person who proposes to make an application for an Access Order.

(4) Any agreement, whenever made, shall be void if and to the extent that it would, apart from this subsection, prevent a person from applying for an Access Order or restrict his right to do so.

Registration of Access Orders and of applications for such orders.

5. (1) In Section 6(1) of the [1972 c. 61] Land Charges Act 1972 (which specifies the writs and orders affecting land that may be entered in the register) after paragraph (c) there shall be added—

“(d) any Access Order under the Access to Neighbouring Land Act 1992.”

(2) In Section 49 of the [1925 c. 21] Land Registration Act 1925 (rules to provide for certain rights, interests and claims to be protected by notice) in Subsection (1) (which specifies those rights, interests and claims) after paragraph (h) there shall be added—

“(i) Access Orders under the Access to Neighbouring Land Act 1992 which, notwithstanding Section 59 of this Act, it may be deemed expedient to protect by notice instead of by caution.”

(3) In Section 64 of that Act (production of certificates for noting on certain dealings etc.) after Subsection (6) there shall be added—

“(7) Subsection (1) above shall also not require the production of the land certificate or of any charge certificate when a person applies for the registration of a notice in respect of an Access Order under the Access to Neighbouring Land Act 1992.”

(4) In any case where—

(a) an Access Order is discharged under Section 6(1)(a) below, and

(b) the order has been protected by an entry registered under the [1972 c. 61] Land Charges Act 1972 or by a notice or caution under the [1925 c. 21] Land Registration Act 1925,

the court may by order direct that the entry, notice or caution shall be cancelled.

(5) The rights conferred on a person by or under an Access Order are not capable of constituting an overriding interest within the meaning of the [1925 c. 21] Land Registration Act 1925, notwithstanding that he or any other person is in actual occupation of the whole or any part of the servient land in question.

(6) An application for an Access Order shall be regarded as a pending land action for the purposes of the [1972 c. 61] Land Charges Act 1972 and the [1925 c. 21] Land Registration Act 1925.

Variation of orders and damages for breach.

6. (1) Where an Access Order or an order under this subsection has been made, the court may, on the application of any party to the proceedings in which the order was made or of any other person on whom the order is binding—

(a) discharge or vary the order or any of its terms or conditions;
(b) suspend any of its terms or conditions; or
(c) revive any term or condition suspended under paragraph (b) above;

and in the application of Subsections (1) and (2) of Section 4 above in relation to an Access Order, any order under this subsection which relates to the Access Order shall be treated for the purposes of those subsections as included in the Access Order.

(2) If any person contravenes or fails to comply with any requirement, term or condition imposed upon him by or under this Act, the court may, without prejudice to any other remedy available, make an order for the payment of damages by him to any other person affected by the contravention or failure who makes an application for relief under this subsection.

Jurisdiction over, and allocation of, proceedings.

7. (1) The High Court and the County Courts shall both have jurisdiction under this Act.

(2) In article 4 of the [S.I. 1991/724] High Court and County Courts Jurisdiction Order 1991 (which provides that proceedings in which the County Courts and the High Court both have jurisdiction may, subject to articles 5 and 6, be commenced either in a County Court or in the High Court) for the words "and 6" there shall be substituted the words ", 6 and 6A" and after article 6 of that order there shall be inserted—

"6A. Applications under Section 1 of the Access to Neighbouring Land Act 1992 shall be commenced in a County Court."

(3) The amendment by Subsection (2) above of provisions contained in an order shall not be taken to have prejudiced any power to make further orders revoking or amending those provisions.

Interpretation and application.

8 (1) Any reference in this Act to an "entry" upon any servient land includes a reference to the doing on that land of anything necessary for carrying out the works to the dominant land which are reasonably necessary for its preservation; and "enter" shall be construed accordingly.

(2) This Act applies in relation to any obstruction of, or other interference with, a right over, or interest in, any land as it applies in relation to an entry upon that land; and "enter" and "entry" shall be construed accordingly.

(3) In this Act—

"Access Order" has the meaning given by Section 1(1) above;

"applicant" means a person making an application for an Access Order and, subject to Section 4 above, "the respondent" means the respondent, or any of the respondents, to such an application;

"the court" means the High Court or a County Court;

"the dominant land" and "the servient land" respectively have the meanings given by Section 1(1) above, but subject, in the case of servient land, to Section 2(1) above;

"land" does not include a highway;

"the specified works" means the works specified in the Access Order in pursuance of Section 2(1)(a) above.

Appendix 1: Access to Neighbouring Land Act 1992 — Text of the Statute

Short title, commencement and extent.

9. (1) This Act may be cited as the Access to Neighbouring Land Act 1992.

(2) This Act shall come into force on such day as the Lord Chancellor may by order made by statutory instrument appoint.

(3) This Act extends to England and Wales only.

Appendix 2

S62 Law of Property Act 1925

Extract from the Law of Property Act 1925
Section 62 -

(1) A conveyance of land shall be deemed to include and shall by virtue of this Act operate to convey, with the land, all buildings, erections, fixtures, commons, hedges, ditches, fences, ways, waters, watercourses, liberties, privileges, easements, rights, and advantages whatsoever, appertaining or reputed to the land, or any part thereof, or, at the time of conveyance, demised, occupied, or enjoyed with, or reputed or known as part or parcel of or appurtenant to the land or any part thereof

(2) A conveyance of land, having houses or other buildings thereon, shall be deemed to include and shall by virtue of this Act operate to convey, with the land, houses, or other buildings, all outhouses, erections, fixtures, cellars, areas, courts, courtyards, cisterns, sewers, gutters, drains, ways, passages, lights, watercourses, liberties, privileges, easements, rights, and advantages whatsoever, appertaining or reputed to appertain to the land, houses, or other buildings conveyed, or any of them, or any part thereof, or, at the time of conveyance, demised, occupied, or enjoyed with, or reputed or known as part or parcel of or appurtenant to, the land, houses or other buildings conveyed, or any of them, or any part thereof.

(3) A conveyance of a manor shall be deemed to include and shall by virtue of this Act operate to convey, with the manor, all pastures, feedings, wastes, warrens, commons, mines, minerals, quarries, furzes, trees, woods, underwoods, coppices, and the ground and soil

thereof, fishings , fisheries, fowlings, courts leet, courts baron, and other courts, view of frank pledge and all that to view of frank pledge doth belong, mills, mulctures, customs, tolls, duties, reliefs, heriots, fines, sums of money, amerciaments, waifs, estrays, chief-rents, quitrents, rentscharge, rents seck, rents of assize, fee farm rents, services, royalties jurisdictions, franchises, liberties, privileges, easements, profits, advantages, rights, emoluments, and hereditaments whatsoever, to the manor appertaining or reputed to appertain, or, at the time of conveyance, demised, occupied, or enjoyed with the same, or reputed or known as part, parcel, or member thereof.

For the purposes of this subsection the right to compensation for manorial incidents on the extinguishment thereof shall be deemed to be a right appertaining to the manor.

(4) This section applies only if and as far as a contrary intention is not expressed in the conveyance, and has effect subject to the terms of the conveyance and to the provisions therein contained.

(5) This section shall not be construed as giving to any person a better title to any property, right, or thing in this section mentioned than the title which the conveyance gives to him to the land or manor expressed to be conveyed, or as conveying to him any property, right, or thing in this section mentioned, further or otherwise than as the same could have been conveyed to him by the conveying parties.

(6) This section applies to conveyances made after the thirty-first day of December, eighteen hundred and eighty-one.

Appendix 3

Extracts from the Law Commission Report No. 151 on Rights of Access to Neighbouring Land

Improvements and alterations

4.8 We do not think that the access scheme should extend to improvements and alterations done for their own sake, since they would not be reasonably necessary for the preservation of land, whereas access under the scheme would be limited to cases where the works were so necessary. On the other hand, we see no reason why the scheme should exclude improvements and alterations which are merely incidental to necessary preservation work. For example, if a window has to be replaced, it should be permissible to replace it with a better one: apart from anything else, an improvement of this sort may reduce the need for access in the future. We suggested in our working paper that such improvements and alterations should be treated as "preservation work" and this was generally accepted by those who wrote to us.

Demolition and rebuilding

4.9 Another matter raised in our working paper was whether the work for which access under our scheme should be available might include demolition and rebuilding. An example might occur where a building had become altogether unsafe or had deteriorated (perhaps because access had not previously been available) to a point at which rebuilding was the only course practicable. Such access would not be required in order to preserve the particular building that was to be demolished. It would, however, facilitate the doing of the next best thing - putting the structure in at least the state of repair that could have been achieved had it been practicable to use the right of access to preserve the old building.

4.10 Most of those who wrote to us about this point agreed that access for demolition should be covered by our scheme; the point was made that demolition is often an essential element of repair. There was less argument as to the rebuilding of a structure following its demolition. Some people were concerned that a right to rebuild could amount to a "developers' charter", or to a means whereby A could secure the construction of a building that would permanently damage B's enjoyment of his own property. The point was also made that, once a building had been demolished under a right of access given by the scheme, no further right of access should be available to assist in its rebuilding, since the new building should be designed without the need for access.

4.11 In the result we recommend that the works for which access should be available under our scheme should include the total or partial demolition of a structure. This is justifiable, not merely in the interests of removing unsafe buildings, but also because preservation work must at times involve an element of demolition, perhaps no more than removing a rusted gutter. Although we are conscious of the arguments against using the scheme for rebuilding structures following their demolition, it is clear that it must cover some rebuilding following demolition because, in the same way as preservation work must sometimes involve demolition of gutters, roofs, etc., it must equally involve their repair or replacement. We therefore recommend that the scheme should permit access for rebuilding or replacement work following demolition, but only if the work involved would amount to preservation work. Accordingly, access under the scheme for the rebuilding of a house or other building following its total demolition would not normally be authorised, since it would be unlikely to amount to preservation work. The purpose of making this distinction is to prevent the scheme being used for major building works that are to be carried out, not in the interests of preservation, but merely in order to develop a site.

Non-structures

4.12 Preservation work is normally related to structures. But it is clear from comments of those who responded to the working paper that access rights are also needed in connection with other property. The example most often mentioned in these comments is the dangerous tree which, while growing on A's land, cannot be lopped or removed without access to B's land. Other examples are the hedge that needs clipping and the ditch, drain or sewer that needs unblocking. The sort of preservation work for which access to non-structures would be available would be similar to that applicable to structures, so that access could, for example, be made available for the removal of a hedge and the planting of a replacement. Since any of these operations may be required to preserve A's land, we recommend that the scheme should apply to non-structures as well as to structures.

Ancillary

4.13 We suggested in our working paper that the right of access, if granted by the court, should be capable of extending to anyone reasonably assisting A in connection with the work. It would, for example, enable his contractors to enter B's land. We also suggested that the right of access should include a right, while the work was going on, to place on B's land any materials and equipment needed in the course of the work, as well as any thing emanating from the work - for example, rubble from a wall which is demolished or branches from a tree which is felled. Our suggestions were confirmed by the consultation; we therefore recommend that a right of access should, unless the court directs otherwise, include these ancillary rights.

General power to make conditions

4.28 In our working paper we provisionally concluded that the court should have a general power to impose conditions on the making of any Access Order, with a view to minimising B's inconvenience and loss of privacy; to reducing security risks and the risks of financial loss or of physical damage or personal injury; to ensuring that the work was done properly and quickly; and to awarding compensation if appropriate. There was general agreement among those who wrote to us that the court should have such a power and we so recommend, though we propose that the generality of the power should be so expressed as to restrict its exercise to the objectives mentioned above; and the power should be exercisable only in so far as the need to achieve those objectives arises from the exercise of the entry made possible by the Access Order. The "conditions" we have in mind fall into three categories:-

(a) those which, unless expressly excluded by the terms of the order, impose certain obligations on the party concerned;
(b) those which are essential features of any Access Order, but which must nevertheless be expressly stated because their precise terms will vary from case to case; and
(c) those which will attach only if expressly imposed by the court at the request of a party.

Making good

4.30 This condition is that the property entered should, so far as is reasonably practicable, be fully reinstated and any damage made good, before the expiry of A's right to enter the property.

4.31 In our working paper we suggested that this should be an automatic condition which would attach in every case unless expressly excluded. Although there may be occasions on which "making good", in the sense of restoring the land to its previous state, will be either undesirable or impracticable, we are satisfied that our provisional conclusion was right, though it would, perhaps, be more accurate to describe what is envisaged as an obligation imposed on A by virtue of an Access Order, unless expressly excluded by that order. We recommend that there should be such an obligation.

Compensation for physical damage

4.50 Nobody who responded to the working paper disagreed with the proposition that compensation should be payable for physical damage to B's property (as distinct from consequential financial loss) caused by the exercise of a right of access under an order. We find it difficult to envisage any circumstances in which it would be right for such compensation not to be payable, and we therefore recommend that the making of an order should carry with it an obligation to pay compensation for physical damage unless such an obligation is expressly excluded.

New respondents

4.74 A is unlikely, in practice, to have difficulty in ascertaining who is the right person to make respondent to his proceedings. Attempts to obtain an informal agreement for access will normally have revealed who is likely to object and only rarely will A need to look beyond the occupier although, if major building work is involved, A will, if prudent, enquire more closely to ascertain whether there is anyone other than B who could require him to stop. However, despite his enquiries, A may, having obtained his Access Order, discover that there is such a person. To meet this contingency, we recommend that

A should be able to apply to the court, at any time before completion of the work, for such a person to be joined as respondent and thus be bound by the order.

4.75 It is, however, very much in A's interests to identify all possible objectors at the outset so that they can all be bound by the order. For, whilst A can apply after the order has been made, for a "newcomer" to be joined as respondent, there is no guarantee that the court will either extend the order to bind the newcomer or, if the newcomer in the meantime starts proceedings against A in trespass, order that those proceedings be stayed pending the joinder application. Further, the newcomer may choose to end A's trespass by exercising his right of self-help: in other words, provided that he uses no more force than is reasonably necessary, he may eject both A and his equipment. This would, to say no more, be inconvenient for A especially if he had already assembled men and equipment. One solution to this problem would be to suspend the newcomer's right of self-help pending a court application. However, this would be difficult to enforce (especially if the newcomer were unaware of the existence of the Access Order) and would be inconsistent with our policy of not binding non-parties. A is really in no different position from that of a contractual licensee who has failed to ensure that everyone entitled to keep him off the land has been made a party to the licence. A should therefore be circumspect at the outset. If, despite his efforts, a newcomer does appear and threatens to eject him and his equipment, A would no doubt be well advised in practice to cease using the access until the newcomer had been joined as a respondent. This would at least reduce the risk of physical confrontation.

Variation etc.

4.76 We recommend that the court should have power, on the application of any party to access proceedings, to vary, suspend or discharge an Access Order (or any term or condition of an Access Order) in the light of any change in circumstances.

Jurisdiction

4.88 We now consider the question of which court or tribunal should have jurisdiction in access proceedings.

4.89 In the working paper we explained that many of the access cases likely to arise would involve simple (but perhaps urgent) questions about work of no great cost arising between ordinary householders of modest means. Accordingly, the tribunal should be local and accessible and its procedure speedy and economical. We also pointed out that some of the cases would be of greater complexity. We suggested that the choice of tribunal lay between the courts and the Lands Tribunal.

4.90 So far as the courts were concerned, we thought that the most appropriate would be the County Court and the High Court. The County Court seemed particularly suitable as regards speed, cost and accessibility. As regards the Lands Tribunal, we noted its expertise in determining a wide range of questions relating to valuation, compensation and the discharge or modification of restrictive covenants. But we pointed out the drawback that the Tribunal had no local offices where informal advice could be obtained, proceedings instituted and interlocutory work handled; also, it was less well-known than the County Court. On balance we thought that the County Court was probably the best available forum for deciding access cases. But we invited comments on the point.

Appendix 3 — Extracts from the Law Commission Report No. 151 on Rights of Access to Neighbouring Land

4.91 Those who wrote to us with their comments expressed a clear preference for the County Court over the Lands Tribunal. There was plainly a greater familiarity with County Court (as opposed to Lands Tribunal) practice and procedure. We have also considered the possibility of arbitration. But we, like many of those who commented, think that the conclusive argument in favour of the County Courts and the High Court is that they have at their disposal comprehensive machinery for enforcing their orders. We accordingly recommend that the County Court should have primary jurisdiction in respect of access applications. We are much fortified in this conclusion by the knowledge that the Council on Tribunals, whose views must carry much weight, agree.

4.92 On the assumption that the County Court should have jurisdiction over access proceedings, we sought views as to the extent of that jurisdiction. It might be desirable for some cases - perhaps the largest and most complicated - to be considered by the High Court. But it was difficult to see what criterion could be used to limit the County Court's jurisdiction in such cases. A criterion based on the likely cost of the proposed work, or on the rateable value of either of the properties involved, would create anomalies and would be difficult to operate in practice. So we suggested that it might be better to give the County Court an unlimited and exclusive jurisdiction, coupled with a power to transfer cases to the High Court.

4.93 Those who wrote to us were in general agreement that the County Court should have an initial unlimited and exclusive jurisdiction in access proceedings, with power for the proceedings to be transferred to the High Court. We agree and so recommend. We did consider the possibility of giving the High Court an initial jurisdiction in cases where all the parties agreed to it. They might do this to avoid expense if, because of the complexity of the case, it seemed inevitable that the case would have, if started in a County Court, to be transferred to the High Court. There would be some merit in this; however, prior agreement of the parties as a basis of jurisdiction presents problems and the additional expense of an agreed transfer to the High Court is not great. Accordingly, we recommend that all access proceedings should be started in the County Court, subject to a power of transfer to the High Court if some important question of law or fact is likely to arise.

The effect of the order

4.106 An Access Order will have the effect of giving A, as against B, a right to enter B's land (and to bring on to it any necessary equipment, etc.). It would not bind anyone other than a respondent. Since the entry would be deemed to be with B's consent, A would therefore be immune from any proceedings based only on entry in accordance with the order brought by B but would enjoy no additional immunity (save immunity from an action in nuisance at the suit of an easement owner who had been made a respondent). B would be required to permit A to enjoy the access specified in the order together with any other rights attached to the order. The right of access given by the order would be subject to any terms or conditions included in it as well as to any undertakings given to the court by or on behalf of any party. The order would cease to have effect on the date specified in it. A respondent's right to enforce any terms and conditions subject to which the order was granted would not be prejudiced by its ceasing to have effect.

Appendix 3 — Extracts from the Law Commission Report No. 151 on Rights of Access to Neighbouring Land

Trespass ab initio[1]

4.111 In the working paper we referred to the rule stated in the *Six Carpenters' Case* to the effect that:

> *where a person having entered upon land under an authority given by law subsequently abuses that authority he becomes a trespasser ab initio, his misconduct relating back so as to make his original entry tortious.*

We suggested that this rule might be expressly negatived for the purposes of the access scheme, since it seemed inappropriate in the context of a scheme designed specifically to ensure that A's entry on B's land was lawful. We thought that there might be a risk that this rule, while operating only in cases of positive misfeasance, might have effect so as retrospectively to render unlawful A's entry pursuant to an Access Order if he exceeded the authority given him by the order or acted in breach of a condition which it imposed. In the event, however, it has proved unnecessary for us to recommend that the rule be negatived. This is because the rule operates only in cases where the defendant enters land under an authority given by law, and not in any case where he enters with the authority or consent of the plaintiff: under the access scheme which we recommend, A's entry upon neighbouring land is deemed to be with B's consent. So the trespass *ab initio* rule will not apply to A's access pursuant to an Access Order.

[1] From the beginning

Appendix 4

Order 49 – Rule 1 of the County Court Supplementary Rules (information to be included in an application)

(1) In this rule, "the 1992 Act" means the Access to Neighbouring Land Act 1992, a section referred to by number means the section so numbered in the 1992 Act and expressions which are defined in the 1992 Act have the same meaning in this rule as they have in that Act.

(2) An application for an Access Order under Section 1 of the 1992 Act shall be made by the issue of a claim form which shall be filed in the court for the district in which the dominant land is situated.

(3) The application shall: -

(a) Identify the dominant land and the servient land and state whether the dominant land is or includes residential land;

(b) Specify the works alleged to be necessary for the preservation of the whole or a part of the dominant land;

(c) State why entry upon the servient land is required and specify the area to which access is required by reference, if possible, to a plan annexed to the application;

(d) Give the name of the person who will be carrying out the works if it is known at the time of the application;

(e) State the proposed date on which, or the dates between which, the works are to be started and their approximate duration, and

(f) State what (if any) provision has been made by way of insurance in the event of possible injury to persons or damage to property arising out of the proposed works.

Appendix 4 — Order 49 – Rule 1 of the County Court Supplementary Rules (information to be included in an application)

(4) The respondents shall be the owner and the occupier of the servient land and any respondent who wishes to be heard on the application shall file an answer within 14 days after the date of service of the application on him.

(5) Order 24, rule 3 shall apply with the necessary modifications to service of the claim form under this rule.

(6) The court may direct that a copy of the claim form shall be served on any person who may be affected by the proposed entry and any such person may, within 14 days after service of the claim form on him, apply to be made a respondent to the application.

(7) The application may be heard and determined by the district judge and may, if the court thinks fit, be dealt with in private.

Appendix 5

Definitions and Interpretations

Access Order – This is the order, which if made by the court, permits the applicant to carry out the works specified in the Access Order.

Adjacent or adjoining land - A distinction is drawn between "adjacent" and "adjoining". Adjacent includes places close to or nearby and the meaning given to the word will depend upon the circumstances. Adjoining means physically contiguous.

In the case of *English Clays Lovering Pochin & Co Ltd v Plymouth Corporation* 1974 there were two areas of land, two miles apart, but joined together by a 25 ft wide strip of land along which ran a pipeline. It was held in this case that the two areas of land were not adjacent to each other although connected by the strip of land.

Agent - An agent is a person who has the authority, express or implied to act on behalf of another, and who agrees to act.

In the case of *Pole v Leask* 1863 it was stated that no one can become another person's agent without the will of that other person. This may be given in writing, orally or implied by the actions/conduct of the principal. The burden of proof lies with the person carrying on business with the assumed agent. This person must prove that the agency existed and that the assumed agent had the required authority. Anyone dealing with someone as an assumed agent should check with the assumed agent's principal that the agency does exist and also the extent of that agency.

Applicant – The applicant is the person applying to the court for an Access Order. It is unnecessary for the applicant to be the owner of the dominant land or to have any interest in it. As long as the applicant has authority to do the required work he can apply for the Access Order.

Associates - are any persons authorised by the applicant to exercise the power of entry conferred by the Access Order.

Building or other structure – Although these words are referred to separately in the Act, every building is a structure.

In the case of *Hobday v Nicol* 1944 it was decided by the Court of Appeal that a row of galvanized iron tanks, filled with earth, and kept in position by their own weight, and put along the edge of a riverbank to try and prevent flooding, was a structure and as such it breached a bye law prohibiting the placing of structures along river banks.

Dominant land – This is the land which is owned and/or occupied by the applicant.

Entry – includes the doing of anything necessary for the carrying out of those works which are reasonably necessary for the preservation of the dominant land.

Forthwith – A direction stating that something must be done forthwith or immediately means that it must be carried out as quickly as possible. The particular circumstances of each case and the nature of the act to be carried out will be taken into account as the following cases illustrate. However, if no harm is caused, forthwith means "at any reasonable time thereafter".

In the case of Re: Southam, ex parte Lamb 1881 local Solicitors instructed London agents to enter an appeal against a Bankruptcy Order on behalf of their client. The appeal was lodged by the London agents with the Registrar of Appeals on the last day on which an appeal could be lodged. The following day (a Friday) they sent a copy of the appeal notice to the local Solicitors, but this was not received until the Monday. The local Solicitors immediately sent the notice to the local County Court. However it was held that the copy of the notice had not been sent to the County Court "forthwith" as required by Rule 144 of the 1870 Bankruptcy Rules. The appeal was therefore out of time. A similar situation arose in the later case of Re: Muscovitch ex parte, Muscovitch 1939 which also involved an appeal against a Bankruptcy Order. An appeal was lodged just 8 days after a Bankruptcy Order but it was held that the copy of the notice of appeal had not been sent "forthwith".

In *Sameen v Abeyewickrema* 1963 a Defendant lodged an appeal on a Friday but did not send with it a notice of security in respect of the respondents' cost of appeal, which he filed on the following Monday. The respondents then contended that the notice of security had not been filed with the court "forthwith" upon the appeal being received by the District Court. The Supreme Court initially agreed with this contention. On appeal to the Board it was held that "forthwith" indicated that the notice should be filed as soon as practicable, depending on the circumstances. In this case the respondents had not been materially affected by the fact that the notice of security had been filed late.

In *Hillingdon London Borough v Cutler* 1968 a local Housing Authority made a Demolition Order under the Housing Act 1957 in connection with some houses that were unfit for human habitation. The initial time and place notices were served on the various owners, but for a variety of reasons the Demolition Order was not made until 12 months later. Section 17 of the Housing Act 1957 states "... the local authority shall forthwith make a Demolition Order ...." One of the property owners on receiving a claim from the local authority to recover the costs of demolition, contended that the Demolition Orders were invalid as they had not been made forthwith. It was held that even if the Demolition Orders were not made forthwith, no detriment had been caused to the owner, but in any event forthwith only means within a reasonable time thereafter.

Appendix 5 — Definitions and Interpretations

Garden - A garden is "a substantially homogenous area, substantially devoted to the growth of fruits, flowers and vegetables" In *Methuen-Campbell v Walters* 1979 it was decided that where there is a cultivated garden which is separated from an adjoining piece of rough pasture, (in this case a paddock) the rough pasture cannot be regarded as part of the garden.

Land - The Act does not apply to land owned by the Crown. The Act gives no definition of land save that highways are excluded and so the definition of land given in Section 1 of the Interpretation Act applies. This states "land includes buildings or other structures, land covered with water and any estate, interest, easement, servitude or right in and over land". The definition is wide enough to extend to a party wall.

In the case of *Dean v Walker* 1996 party wall issues were raised. This case was actually brought under the Access to Neighbouring Land Act 1992 and details can be found in Appendix 7.

Likely – has been construed so as to mean a "reasonable prospect" of something happening and "it's more probable than not".

The case of *Dunning v Board of Governors of the United Liverpool Hospitals* 1973 involved disclosure of hospital records. Section 31 of the Administration of Justice Act 1970 allows an order to be made for discovery of documents, when at the time the application comes before the court there are grounds for thinking "it likely" that court proceedings will follow. According to Lord Denning the word likely should be construed as meaning "may" or "may well be made" depending on the outcome of the discovery.

Mainly – Generally speaking the word "mainly" probably means "more than half".

In *Berthelemy v Neale* 1952 which was a case brought under Section 10(1) of the Leasehold Property (temporary provisions) Act 1951 a tenant wished to renew the lease on his shop. In order to benefit from the protection of the Act the tenant had to prove that he was running a shop. The Act describes a shop as "premises occupied wholly for business purposes, and so occupied wholly or mainly for the purposes of a retail trade or business". The problem which the tenant had was that 90% of the products which he sold, were sold wholesale and not retail. However the whole property was used from time to time to produce items for retail sale. The County Court refused to grant a new tenancy. The case then went to the Court of Appeal who upheld this decision on the basis that it is not how much of the premises is used for retail purposes, but how much of the business is actually a retail business. In this case only about 10% could be classed as retail sales.

Obstruction – Obstruction need not amount to actual physical violence. Anything that makes it more difficult or awkward for someone to carry out the job in hand can amount to obstruction.

In *Borrow v Howland* 1896 a gentleman refused to allow dustmen into his house to remove his rubbish. Whilst he had not threatened the dustmen with physical violence his refusal to allow them access amounted to wilful obstruction.

Occupier - A person is an occupier if he has influence over the activities of others using the property and a degree of control over the state of the property. In order to be an occupier a person does not have to have control over the whole of the property which he may share with others. An Occupier includes a person who has a licence to occupy. A statutory tenant can also be regarded as an Occupier. It is doubtful that a person who entered the property unlawfully, for instance a trespasser, would be regarded as an Occupier.

In *Wheat v E Lacon & Co* Ltd 1966 various forms of occupation were considered. In this case the following statements were made in relation to an occupier:

a) that two people may be occupiers of the same premises at the same time
b) the occupier is he who has the immediate supervision and control and the power of permitting or prohibiting the entry of other persons
c) if a person has any degree of control over the state of the premises it is enough and can amount to occupation.

In the case of *Stevens v London Borough of Bromley* 1972 the Plaintiff developed some land as a caravan site without planning permission. He then sold some of the caravans as permanent residences and charged ground rent to the caravan dwellers. The local planning authority served an enforcement notice requiring him to stop using the land as a caravan site. Notice was served on the Plaintiff as owner and occupier of the land and the other caravan dwellers were also served with notice on various different dates. The Plaintiff argued that the notice was invalid as it had been served on owners and occupiers on different dates. The Planning authority argued that caravan dwellers were not occupiers, but licensees, and therefore service on the caravan dwellers was unnecessary in any event. It was found that the caravan dwellers were licensees and also occupiers. Although they were licensees, in addition they were occupiers of the plots on which their caravans stood.

In *Woodcock v South Western Electricity Board* 1975 squatters occupied a property without the knowledge or consent of the owners. It was held that occupiers did not include a person whose original entry was unlawful and forcible.

The case of *Brown v Ministry of Housing and Local Government* 1953 involved statutory tenants. Under the Acquisition of Land (Authorisation Procedure) Act 1946 notice of the Compulsory Purchase Order must be given to every statutory tenant of land affected by the order. The applicants were statutory tenants under the Rent Restrictions Act which afforded the tenants protection from eviction and lived in two flats in the same house. As no notices had been served on them they were not aware of the public enquiry which had been held and therefore did not have the opportunity to object. They asked the court to quash the compulsory purchase order. The respondents argued that they did not have to serve notice on statutory tenants. The compulsory purchase orders were quashed

Preservation – includes works of maintenance or repair. Actual development is not permitted.

Respondent – The respondent is the owner and/or occupier of the servient land. Other parties may be joined as respondents if necessary (e.g. respondent's mortgage provider). Only persons who are a party to the Access Order are bound by it.

Residential Land - If work is required to a flat over a shop (for example, repairs to the exterior wall of flat) this would be regarded as work to residential land and as such compensation does not become an issue under the Act. However any work to the actual shop would be classed as commercial and compensation would become an issue.

Servant – In the main a servant is a person who takes orders from his master, including the work he has to do, and the way in which the job is to be carried out.

Servient land - In most cases the servient land will be owned and/or occupied by the respondent.

Specified works – Are the works set out in the Access Order.

Substantially more difficult - The Act provides that the applicant must show that it is not possible to do the works or that the works would be substantially more difficult without access over the respondent's land. Substantial has been construed to mean "considerable". Substantially has been found to mean neither trivial nor total.

The case of *Granada Theatres v Freehold Investments (Leytonstone)* 1958 involved a dispute between a landlord and tenant over the exact meaning of "structural repairs of a substantial nature". It was held that the repairs were considerable and therefore substantial.

The case of *R v Lloyd* 1967 involved mental health issues in connection with diminished responsibility and the exact extent thereof. The trial judge stated that the word "substantially" did not mean total.

Trespass – Entry pursuant to an Access Order cannot be regarded as a trespass. The entry will be regarded as authorised as long as it is in accordance with the Access Order.

Appendix 6

Checklists

Applicant's Checklist: -

Please note these checklists are by no means exhaustive, as the information required, and the steps to be taken, will vary depending upon individual circumstances.

Main points to consider when access is required over neighbouring property to carry out maintenance works to residential land which will take days rather than months to complete (e.g. repointing wall, replacing guttering).

1. Check your title deeds as they may contain a right to go on to your neighbour's land for maintenance purposes. If not:

2. Consider the work which you wish to do.

    a) How long will it take?
    b) How much inconvenience is this going to cause your neighbour?
    c) What steps can you take to minimise the inconvenience to your neighbour?
    d) What equipment do you need to take on to your neighbour's land?

    Take five minutes to view the situation from your neighbour's point of view. What would you require if the shoe was on the other foot?

3. Armed with the above information go and ask your neighbour if he could do you a favour by allowing you to go on to his land so that you may carry out your repair work. See if you can discuss it over a cup of tea, or something stronger. When a request such as this is

put across in a friendly and polite way very few people will refuse. However if you happen to be one of those unlucky people, whose neighbour goes out of his way to be difficult - read on.

4. If your neighbour refuses to give you access, follow this up with a very polite letter setting out your access requirements and the steps you are prepared to take to minimise upset and disturbance to your neighbour. Ask him if he could possibly reconsider the situation. If you end up in court it will do your case no harm, if you can show that you have bent over backwards to accommodate your neighbour. Keep a copy of the letter you have written to your neighbour, and his reply, if you receive one. If access is still refused:

5. Check whether your particular circumstances meet the criteria laid down by the Act:-

   a) Is the work you wish to carry out reasonably necessary for the preservation of your property? Only works of maintenance and repair are covered by the Act - the building of an extension would be excluded.

   b) Is there any other way you can do the work without access to your neighbour's land? If there is another way, give this some serious consideration rather than relying on the Act. An Access Order will only be granted if work cannot be carried out, or would be substantially more difficult to carry out, without access to your neighbour's land.

   c) Consider how much inconvenience and disturbance your neighbour is going to suffer as a result of the work you wish to carry out. Is it reasonable to expect your neighbour to put up with this? Remember the court has a discretion to refuse an Access Order if the inconvenience and hardship to your neighbour would be too great.

6. If after considering the above you still wish to proceed you will need to start putting your case together by taking the following steps: -

7. Give your neighbour one last chance to agree to access. Grit your teeth and write one more polite letter to your neighbour. Indicate in this letter that you really would like to come to some amicable arrangement, but if agreement cannot be reached, you will reluctantly have to apply for an Access Order under the Access to Neighbouring Land Act 1992.

   a) Call into or phone your local County Court. Ask them for three copies of the N208 Claim Form (CPR Part 8). These can be obtained free of charge. At the same time check the amount of the court fee payable (this is presently £120.00). Bear in mind that an Access Order must be applied for in the County Court covering the district in which the dominant land (your property) is situated.

   b) Obtain a copy of an Ordnance Survey Map showing your property and that of your neighbour. This can usually be obtained from the Land Registry or your local friendly estate agent. Mark on this plan the boundaries of your property and the full extent of the property owned by your neighbour. You should also mark on this plan the area of your neighbour's property over which you require access. Double-check your plan. Have you included all the land over which you need access? Have you perhaps overlooked an alleyway? Does all the land over which you require access belong to just one person?

   c) Is your neighbour the only one you need to name as the respondent in your application for an Access Order? This should be fairly straightforward if he is the owner and occupier of the property over which you require access. Is there anyone else that can prevent you having access? If so, you should ensure that they do not object to you having access. If they do object you should also name them as respondent in your application. For further details refer to the Observations on Section 1.

d) Prepare a schedule of the work which you require to carry out, together with a list of the plant and machinery which you will need to complete the job. Calculate how long the job will take you, and build yourself a little leeway in case of poor weather or other unforeseen circumstances. Check that you have insurance cover in case you injure someone or cause damage to your neighbour's property as a result of your work.

e) Finally complete your claim form, giving as much information as you can, broadly following the precedent in Appendix 9. You will need three copies of your claim form and plan. One claim form is for your records, another for the court and the third copy for the respondent. If there is more than one respondent, you will need to provide additional copies of the claim form.

Additional checklist if the work which the applicant requires to carry out is work to non-residential land.

1. Where work is required to commercial property, for example a shop, the Act provides that the respondent may be entitled to compensation. The applicant will therefore have to provide figures setting out the financial advantage to him of carrying out the works via the respondent's land. Please refer to the Observations on Section 2 (Subsections (5)(6) and (7)).

2. If your property is a commercial one, I cannot stress the importance of trying to reach agreement with your neighbour without resorting to the Act. If the respondent is awarded compensation by the court, and you are unable or unwilling to pay that compensation you will

not get your access and all your time and efforts in bringing an action under the Access to Neighbouring Land Act 1992 will have been wasted. In all probability it will be cheaper for you to come to some private arrangement with the respondent even if this involves a voluntary payment by you to compensate your neighbour for any inconvenience caused to him whilst you are carrying out your repair work.

Further checks to make when works required are major projects likely to take some months to complete

It may be wise to obtain a copy of your neighbour's title deeds (please refer to the section in Appendix 8 headed "How to find out more information about the servient land"). How much do you know about your neighbour's finances? Is there any chance that a Lender could repossess your neighbour's property? If there is a mortgage on your neighbour's property consider naming the Lender as a respondent. Is it likely that your neighbour could sell his property, either before you get your Access Order, or during the period you are carrying out the work on your property. The steps you can take to register the Access Order are considered in the Chapter headed Observations on Section 5.

Appendix 6 — Checklists

Respondent's Checklist: -

Please note these checklists are by no means exhaustive, as the information required, and the steps to be taken, will vary depending upon individual circumstances.

In all cases it is important to check your title deeds. They may contain a clause giving your neighbour the right to enter upon your property for the purposes of carrying out maintenance work to your neighbour's property. If this is the case you are legally obliged to allow your neighbour access. Do not however confuse a right to enter upon your property for maintenance purposes with a right of way. If your deeds give your neighbour a right of way over your land, that is exactly what your neighbour has - a right of way nothing more. A right of way does not give your neighbour permission to stay on your property for hours on end whilst he carries out repair work to his property, nor does it entitle your neighbour to erect scaffolding etc. Even if you are on good terms with your neighbour it may be wise to agree relevant points from the list below to avoid conflict in the future.

Main points to consider when your land is residential land and you have no objection to your neighbour's application for an Access Order

1. Who will carry out the maintenance work? Will it be your neighbour or a builder? Does your neighbour have the required skill and knowledge to carry out the work properly and efficiently with minimum inconvenience to you? If not, you may wish to stipulate that you want the work carried out by a reputable builder. This will avoid the scenario which I have set out at the end of the chapter containing my Observations on Section 3.

2. Check that your neighbour (or his builder) has adequate insurance against injury to persons and damage to your land which might arise from the work your neighbour wishes to carry out.

3. What precautions do you require your neighbour to take to protect your property? If the work is likely to give rise to rubble and other building waste, sheeting may be required to protect your lawn/plants. Perhaps plants will need to be removed temporarily to prevent them being damaged. Make it clear who is to be responsible for this. Would you prefer to see to this or will it be your neighbour's responsibility?

4. What is to happen to any rubble and other waste arising from the work? Do you want it to be cleared from your property on a daily basis or removed when the work is finished? If it is to be cleared when the work is finished, where will it be stored in the meantime?

5. What equipment and materials will be brought on to your land? Will they be left over night? Where will they be stored when not in use? Is there anything you do not want left on your land e.g. inflammable liquids? Is there anything you do not want brought on to your land at all e.g. scaffolding?

6. When would you prefer the work to be carried out? Consider stating that the work is to be carried out Monday to Friday, and so leaving you in peace at the weekends. Do you wish to stipulate that work must finish by 5.00 p.m. each day so that your evenings are your own. How long is the work going to take to complete?

7. Under this Act compensation can be paid for substantial loss of privacy or other substantial inconvenience. Depending upon the relationship which you have with your neighbour, you may or may not wish to make a claim for this.

8. Make it clear that if any damage occurs to your property, it is to be reinstated to its original condition on completion of the work. Take some photographs of your property before the work begins, so that you have a record of the condition of your property/garden prior to the work commencing. The Act makes provision for the payment

of compensation to cover any loss, damage or injury. Consider asking the court to include in the Access Order a clause allowing for the payment of compensation to cover damage which may be caused. It could be stated in the Access Order that the level of compensation (if any) is to be agreed by an independent expert without the need to go back to court.

9. Is there anyone that you wish to specifically exclude from having access to your property? If so stipulate this.

Main points to consider when your land is residential land and you do object to your neighbour's application for an Access Order

In certain circumstances you can object to your neighbour's application for an Access Order. There are several grounds:-

1. That the works your neighbour wishes to carry out are not reasonably necessary for the preservation of your neighbour's property. Only basic preservation works are covered by the Act. If your neighbour wishes to change the colour of his walls from ghastly green to pretty pink and requires access to your property to complete the repainting of his property the Act will not help him. If on the other hand he has to repoint the walls of his property and then repaint, this would probably be classed as basic preservation work.

   Similarly if your neighbour requires access to your property to complete an extension which he is building, he cannot use the Act to assist him to gain access to his land via your property. The building of a new extension would not be classed as basic preservation work under the Act. Section 1(4) of the Act gives a list of works classed as basic preservation work, although the courts have discretion to include other works not included in this list. The onus is on your neighbour to prove that the work which he wishes to carry out is reasonably necessary for the preservation of his property.

2. If there is another way your neighbour can do the work without access to your property you can object on these grounds. It is not sufficient that it is more convenient for your neighbour to have access over your property to carry out the work. It must be a necessity.

3. You can object on the grounds that if an Access Order were granted to your neighbour you would suffer interference/ disturbance/hardship to such an extent that it would be unreasonable to make an Access Order. The onus is now on you to show that it would be unreasonable for the court to make an Access Order. In this respect you should bear in mind that the court has to carry out a balancing act between the nuisance caused to you if the Access Order is granted and the inconvenience caused to your neighbour if it is not.

Main points to consider when your land is not residential land and is a commercial property

If your property is a commercial one you are entitled to claim consideration and compensation from your neighbour. Please refer to Section 2(5)(6) and (7) for further details.

Appendix 7

Cases brought under the Access to Neighbouring Land Act 1992

Section 1 - Work which comes within this Act can be carried out on any land including a party wall.

Another important point to be established in this case was that the outcome of an application under the Access to Neighbouring Land Act does not in any way affect other disputes between the parties.

MICHAEL DEAN v GEORGE DOYLE WALKER [1996] EWCA 380

This case is a typical example of how disputes between neighbours can escalate and spiral out of control, especially when one of the parties concerned decides to act in person. This case went as far as the Court of Appeal which, at the end of the day, agreed with the initial decision made by the County Court.

Mr. Walker owned a property, the gable end of which was in poor condition and required repointing. To carry out this work Mr. Walker required access to Mr. Dean's property. Mr. Dean's property adjoined the southwest wall of Mr. Walker's property. The gable end wall of Mr. Walker's property extended on all sides beyond the part of the wall forming the eastern wall of Mr. Dean's property and was regarded as a party wall.

The judgement in this case mentions that there were other disputes between Mr. Walker and Mr. Dean which had nothing to do with access, and that Mr. Dean was concerned that if he agreed to Mr. Walker's application for Access, this could jeopardise other disputes which he had with Mr. Walker. It was stated that the outcome of an application under the Access to Neighbouring Land Act would not in any way affect other disputes between Mr. Dean and Mr. Walker.

Appendix 7 — Cases brought under the Access to Neighbouring Land Act 1992

Mr. Walker asked Mr. Dean for access. This access was not forthcoming and Mr. Walker applied to his local County Court for an Access Order allowing him access to Mr. Dean's property to repoint the gable end wall of his house. Mr. Walker's application for an Access Order was successful. The Access Order was made by District Judge Holloway on the 25th October 1994. Mr. Dean, acting in person, appealed against this decision to Her Honour Judge Holt. The basis of Mr. Dean's appeal was that Mr. Walker's application was unnecessary as he had always been willing to allow the work to be carried out. This statement was not supported by the facts. At the earlier hearing before District Judge Holloway Mr. Dean had argued that Mr. Walker should not have an Access Order because;

(a) the gable end wall did not belong to Mr. Walker, and was a party and party wall and therefore the provisions of the Act did not apply.
(b) that the works to be carried out to the wall were not reasonably necessary
(c) if an Access Order were granted Mr. Dean and his wife would suffer great hardship and that it would be unreasonable for an order to be made.

The judgement of Judge Holt indicates that Mr. Dean again put forward the same arguments as those set out above and there is no indication that Mr. Dean was willing to consent to an Access Order.

The judge gave consideration to the status of the gable end wall and stated that she did not have to decide whether or not the Access to Neighbouring Land Act 1992 extended to allowing work on neighbouring land. The Act referred to "any land". Therefore work which came within the Act could be carried out on any land. The judge also found that the works were reasonable necessary and Mr. Dean did not challenge this. Mr. Dean did not proceed further with his claim that he would suffer hardship. The judge made an Access Order in favour of Mr. Walker and Mr. Dean appealed again to the Court of Appeal.

This appeal concentrated on the ownership of the gable end wall. Mr. Dean's first ground of appeal again repeated earlier arguments that the work authorised by the Access Order was work to that part of a party wall which belonged to him, and therefore the judge had no authority under the Act to grant an Access Order authorising work to property belonging to another. Mr. Dean's second ground of appeal was that Mr. Walker did not own that part of the wall to which the work was to be authorised.

The court reminded Mr. Dean that the long title of the Act stated that it was "An Act to enable persons who desire to carry out works to any land which are reasonably necessary for the preservation of that land to obtain access to neighbouring land in order to do so; and for purposes connected therewith." The court also stated that as the Act gave no definition of land it had the meaning given in Schedule 1 of the Interpretation Act 1978 which states "Land includes buildings and other structures, land covered with water, and any estate, interest, easement, servitude or right in or over land." The courts took the view that the definition was wide enough to include a party wall.

In the judgement given by the Court of Appeal it was stated "the fundamental fallacy in Mr. Dean's argument is the proposition that the Access to Neighbouring Land Act does not apply to a party and party wall." The judgement went on to say that both District Judge Holt and Judge Holloway had been right in reaching their conclusions, namely that Mr. Walker was entitled to an Access Order.

Mr. Dean's appeal was dismissed and he was ordered to pay Mr. Walker's costs.

The judgement given by the Court of Appeal runs into 8 pages and can be read in full by visiting the Internet website of the British and Irish Legal Information Institute http://www.bailii.org/

Appendix 7 — Cases brought under the Access to Neighbouring Land Act 1992

Section 2 - Payment of compensation and consideration

A semi-derelict building whose use had once been commercial, but which had planning permission to convert it into a dwelling, was not classed as residential until the conversion had been carried out. It was still classed as commercial and therefore consideration was payable.

COULTON v PICKLES 1995[2]

As far as I can ascertain this unrecorded case was one of the first cases to come before the courts under the Access to Neighbouring Land Act 1992 and involved work to a semi derelict building, which had previously been used as a mill. Mr. and Mrs. Coulton owned this building and wished to convert it into a single dwelling. The rear wall of the mill was in a poor condition and required demolition and rebuilding. The outside of this wall abutted a garden belonging to Mr. Pickles. To facilitate the work the Coultons would need to erect scaffolding in Mr. Pickle's garden. It was estimated that the work to the wall would take about three months to complete.

Both parties agreed that Mr. Coulton, the applicant, was entitled to access under the Act, but could not reach agreement over the sum to be paid to Mr. Pickles, the respondent by way of compensation and consideration. The parties were able to reach agreement on other practical matters relating to access, the type of scaffolding and the work to be carried out.

Under Section 2(4)(i) of the Act the respondent was entitled to compensation for any loss, damage or injury, or under Section 2(4)(ii) any substantial loss of privacy or other substantial inconvenience caused by the applicant and (as this was a non-residential property) consideration under Section 2(5) for the privilege of entering upon the respondent's land in pursuance of the Access Order to carry out the

---

[2]Grateful thanks to Alistair Redler for making material in respect of this case available to the author.

work. The amount of consideration to be calculated by taking into account the likely financial advantage of the order to the applicant and the degree of inconvenience likely to be caused to the respondent.

Under Section 2(4)(i) of the Act the respective parties Surveyors agreed the sum of £90.00 to cover the cost of damage to plants and lawn likely to be damaged by the erection of scaffolding.

The applicant did not feel that there should be any payment under Section 2(4)(ii) as any loss of privacy or inconvenience would not be substantial. If the Access Order was granted the work would be carried out from the respondent's garden with workmen facing away from the respondent's garden whilst they were working on the wall. The applicant was prepared to provide netted scaffolding to restrict dust and debris and which would also act as a visual barrier between the applicant's building and the respondent's garden.

However, if the Access Order was refused the work to the wall would be carried out overhand, with workmen facing the respondent's garden. Whilst the wall was being demolished anyone in the applicant's property would look directly on to the respondent's garden. There would be no netted scaffolding to act as a screen. The respondent eventually agreed that the access and erection of scaffolding would be better from his point of view than if the work was carried out overhand.

The court accepted that the important point was the effect on the respondent as a result of the entry not as a result of the works. If the effect of the entry is to minimise the effect of the works, that would be an improvement to the respondent.

The court also agreed that the respondent would not suffer substantial loss of privacy or substantial inconvenience, but some inconvenience would be caused. The court therefore awarded the sum of £25.00 per week in respect of inconvenience caused due to the loss of the garden.

Another important part of this case was the payment of consideration. Consideration is not payable if the work being carried out by the applicant are works to residential land. The applicant therefore tried to persuade the court that the semi-derelict mill was classed as residential land, and put forward the argument, that whilst the mill had once been classed as an industrial building, planning permission for change of use had been obtained, and when the works had been completed it would be a single dwelling. The court did not accept this and held the proposed work was not work to residential land as the property had been used for commercial purposes and was not yet residential. Consideration therefore came into the equation. The parties agreed that the additional cost of carrying out the work without the Access Order would be about £7,000.00 which sum would be more than the increase in value of the mill as a result of the work. £7,000.00 was therefore calculated to be the likely financial advantage to the applicant of carrying out the work with the benefit of an Access Order.

The court ordered that the amount of the financial advantage should be shared with the respondent on an equal basis, and awarded the respondent £3,500 by way of consideration, despite arguments put forward on behalf of the applicant. To summarise the respondent was awarded:-

£ 90.00	compensation to cover damage to plants and lawn
£ 300.00	compensation for inconvenience (it was estimated the work would take 12 weeks (12 x £25.00 = £300.00).
£3,500	consideration
£3,890	Total payable to respondent

As a result of this judgement the applicant could not afford to pay the respondent the large sum ordered by the court and the property was put back on the market

NOTE

This case came before the courts prior to the Woolf Reforms. It is now hoped that an applicant would not be penalised so harshly in future.

Section 2 - subsection 9 - Unreasonable respondents ordered to pay applicant's costs. Applicant only order to pay cost of one meeting between respondent and their solicitors

***WILLIAMS v EDWARDS AND EDWARDS* [1997] CLYB 561**

Williams (applicant) wanted access to land owned by Edwards (respondents). Williams wished to erect scaffolding on Edwards' land. Initially Edwards agreed to the access requested by Williams and workmen entered onto Edwards' land. The Architects employed by Williams sent Edwards copies of plans and indicated that if they required any further information they could contact the Architect or Williams direct. Edwards did not seek any further information.

Edwards subsequently objected to access. The Builder acting for Williams wrote to Edwards to see if they could discuss the matter. Edwards still refused to agree to access. Williams then wrote several letters to Edwards followed by a letter from his solicitors, and a visit to Edwards home and offices. All to no avail.

An application was reluctantly made by Williams for an Access Order under the Access to Neighbouring Land Act 1992.

Edwards then indicated that they were prepared to agree to access as long as certain conditions were met and in particular that Williams paid Edwards' costs.

Appendix 7 — Cases brought under the Access to Neighbouring Land Act 1992

The Builder acting for Williams confirmed that most of the conditions could be met.

Edwards then tried to add further conditions including a request for a payment into court of £2,000 and Edwards' costs to be paid.

The Builder for Edwards was again able to confirm that the additional conditions could be met, excluding the payment into court and costs.

When the case came before the courts all terms were agreed between the parties, except that there had been no payment into court.

The court held that Edwards had been unreasonable and that Williams had done all he possibly could. Instead of Williams being ordered to pay Edwards' costs the situation was reversed and Edwards were ordered to pay Williams' costs. Edwards were however allowed to claim from Williams the cost of one meeting with a Solicitor for advice.

Appendix 8

How to find out more information about the servient land

It is more likely than not that your neighbour's land/property (the servient land) will be registered at H.M. Land Registry. Provided it is registered, it will have been allocated a specific title number by the Land Registry. Since 1990 any member of the general public has been able to inspect the register and obtain a copy of any registered title. A copy of the register can be obtained through the post or by a personal visit to the appropriate Land Registry.

There are 24 District Land Registries. Each Land Registry Office has a Customer Information Centre. You will find the address of your nearest Land Registry in the phone book.

The Land Registry Forms mentioned in this section can be purchased from any law stationers or downloaded free of charge from the Land Registry's web-site (www.landreg.gov.uk/).

The first step is to find out whether or not your neighbour's land is registered at the Land Registry. An application for an Official Search of the Index Map needs to be made using Land Registry Form 96. To complete this form all you need is the address of your neighbour's land/property or a plan of it. There is a box on this form indicating that a fee is payable. This section of the form can be ignored as the Land Registry no longer make a charge for an Official Search of the Index Map. Once you have completed the form simply send it off to the Land Registry (together with a plan if applicable). Within a few days the Land Registry will send you the result of the search which will usually give you the title number of the property you have searched against, for example CL12345.

Once you know the title number you can apply to the Land Registry for Office Copies of the Register and Title Plan using Land Registry

Appendix 8 — How to find out more information about the servient land

Form 109. Completion of this form is fairly straightforward and there are also guidance notes on the reverse of the form. You need to apply for an office copy of the register and an office copy of the title plan by putting a cross in the first two boxes of Section 3. Send the completed form to the Land Registry together with your cheque for £8.00 made payable to H.M. Land Registry.

The Land Registry will then send you office copies of the register and a copy of the filed plan relating to the property you have searched against. The register is divided into three sections which can briefly be described as: the Property Register which will give the address of the land/property and will refer to the land/property as being edged red on the filed plan; the Proprietorship Register which will give details of the class of title held and the full names of the owners; and the Charges register which will disclose whether there are any mortgages on the property. The office copy of the register may also reveal other information relating to the land/property. Should it be necessary to commence proceedings under the Access to Neighbouring Land Act 1992 a copy of a plan showing the land over which access is required will need to be sent to the court The filed plan supplied by the Land Registry should be sufficient for this purpose.

If the result of the Index Map Search mentioned above, indicates that the land is unregistered, then I am afraid the amount of information readily available will be very limited. You may not be able to find out any more information about your neighbour's land/property than you know already.

Appendix 9

Precedents

Precedent for an application for an Access Order – Plan not included but will be required in any application

Application for an Access Order

Claim Form (CPR Part 8)

Claimant
Derek Ian Young
10 New Street
Nowhere Town
Cornwall

Defendant
Adrian Old
11 New Street
Nowhere Town
Cornwall

Does your claim include any issues under the Human Rights Act 1998 Yes No

Details of claim (see also overleaf)

1. The Claimant claims an Access Order pursuant to Section 1 of the Access to Neighbouring Land Act 1992 requiring the Defendant to allow the Claimant access to his property known as 11 New Street Nowhere Town Cornwall (the servient land) for the purpose of

carrying out certain works reasonably necessary for the preservation of the Claimant's property known as 10 New Street Nowhere Town Cornwall (the dominant land).

2. This claim is made under the Access to Neighbouring Land Act 1992.
3. Part 8 of the Civil Procedure Rules 1998 applies to this claim.
4. The grounds upon which the Claimant claims to be entitled to the order and the particulars required by the Civil Procedure Rules 1998, Schedule 2, CCR Order 49 rule 1 are as follows: -

Defendant's
name and
address

Details of claim (continued)

(a) The Claimant is the owner and occupier of the dominant land as defined in Sections 1 and 8 of the Act which is residential land and is shown edged red on the attached plan.

(b) The Defendant is the owner and occupier of the servient land which is shown edged blue on the attached plan.

(c) The works specified in the schedule below are necessary for the preservation of part of the dominant land and cannot be carried out without entry onto the servient land.

(d) The works cannot be carried out without entry upon that part of the servient land, comprising of an alleyway and garden area, shown coloured yellow on the attached plan for the following reasons:-

(i) The works comprise repointing a wall which is approximately four metres high and which directly abuts the servient land and which is shown hatched brown on the attached plan.

(ii) Access to the wall is impossible without entry upon the servient land.

(iii) The work cannot be carried out without a scaffold tower, cement mixer and wheelbarrow which can only be placed on the servient land.

(iv) The only practicable way to obtain access to the wall and to erect a scaffold tower and for the bringing of the cement mixer and wheelbarrow and for the delivery of materials and thereafter for the removal of waste and rubble lies over the land shown coloured yellow on the attached plan.

(e) The Claimant proposes to carry out the repointing work himself.

(f) The repointing works are intended to start within two weeks of the granting of an Access Order and are expected to continue for 5 days.

(g) The Claimant has effected a policy of insurance with ABC Insurance Company Plc which provides unlimited indemnity in respect of injury to persons or damage to property arising out of the works.

THE SCHEDULE

Remove existing rendering to wall abutting the servient land repoint and generally make good. Remove rubble and waste materials.

DATED

Statement of Truth

*(I believe)(The Claimant believes) that the facts stated in these particulars of claim are true.

* I am duly authorised by the Claimant to sign this statement.

Full name ---

Name of Claimant's solicitor's firm ----------------------------

Signed ---

Position or office held ---

*(Claimant) (Litigation friend)(Claimant's solicitor) (if signing on behalf of firm or company)

**delete as appropriate*

Claimant or Claimant's solicitor's address to which documents should be sent if different from overleaf. If you are prepared to accept service by fax or email please add details

Precedent for an answer to Part 8 Claim Form agreeing to the making of an order but specifying terms and conditions to be imposed upon the Claimant

(Same heading as claim form)

ANSWER

I, Adrian Old of 11 New Street Nowhere Town Cornwall the Defendant to this application say that:

1. I do not oppose the making of an Access Order pursuant to the Access to Neighbouring Land Act 1992.
2. I apply to the court to impose the following terms and conditions on the making of the order: -
   (a) That the Claimant appoints a qualified builder to be approved by me or the court because the Claimant is not a builder and has caused damage to the servient land when he attempted to repoint this wall on a previous occasion.
   (b) That the Claimant's builder takes precautions to ensure my garden is not further damaged by falling rubble and the placing of machinery on the servient land.

(c) That the Claimant's builder effects adequate insurance against injury to persons and damage to the servient land arising from the work.

(d) That the work is only carried out between 9.00 a.m. and 5.00 p.m. Monday to Friday.

(e) That all waste is cleared from the site on a daily basis to minimise damage to the servient land.

(f) That the Claimant's builder ensures that the alleyway is not obstructed at any time.

DATED

Statement of Truth
*(I believe)(The Defendant believes) that the facts stated in this answer are true.
* I am duly authorised by the Defendant to sign this statement

Full name ---

Name of Defendant's solicitor's firm -----------------------

Signed --

Position or office held --

***(Defendant) (Litigation friend)(Defendant's solicitor) (if signing on behalf of firm or company)**

delete as appropriate

Precedent for an answer to Part 8 Claim Form objecting to an Access Order

(Same heading as claim form)

ANSWER

I, Adrian Old of 11 New Street Nowhere Town Cornwall the Defendant to this application say that:

1. I oppose the making of an Access Order pursuant to Section 1 of the Access to Neighbouring Land Act 1992 on the grounds that: -

   (a) I would suffer considerable interference and disturbance in my use and enjoyment of that part of the servient land which comprises my garden to such a degree that it would be unreasonable to make the Access Order. This is due to the fact that over the last 18 months I have worked seven days a week preparing my garden for the Nowhere Town Garden in Bloom Competition. It is crucial that I prepare for this competition without any further disruption, or interference from the Claimant. The competition is scheduled to take place in 9 months time.

   and/or

   (b) The Claimant carried out some re-pointing work on this wall a few months ago and no further works are necessary. The Claimant's real reason for making this application is to cause me further aggravation and irritation and is an act of revenge brought about by an unconnected dispute between us which is the subject of separate court proceedings.

2. If the court grants an Access Order I apply to the court to impose the following terms and conditions:

(Insert relevant details)

DATED

Statement of Truth

*(I believe)(The Defendant believes) that the facts stated in this answer are true.
* I am duly authorised by the Defendant to sign this statement

Full name --

Name of Defendant's solicitor's firm -----------------------

Signed ---

Position or office held ---

***(Defendant) (Litigation friend)(Defendant's solicitor) (if signing on behalf of firm or company)**

delete as appropriate

Precedent for an application to vary the terms of an Access Order

Application to vary an Access Order under the Access to Neighbouring Land Act 1992 to provide for works specified in the Access Order to be carried out at a later date and to include weekend work

(Same heading as claim form)

APPLICATION

This application is made by the Claimant pursuant to Section 6(1) of the Access to Neighbouring Land Act 1992.

The Claimant wishes to apply for an order to vary the terms of the Access Order made in this action on the 1st April 2001 to provide that the work specified in the Access Order may be carried out during a two week period commencing 1st June 2001 instead of the date specified in the Access Order and that for this two week period the condition preventing the specified works being carried out at the weekend be suspended.

The Claimant's contractors are unable to start the work specified in the Access Order until the 1st June 2001. The Claimant's contractors are scheduled to start another job on the 15th June 2001. The only period during which they can fit in the work specified in the Access Order is during the two week period commencing 1st June 2001.

The Claimant will rely upon the following written evidence in support of this application:-

(a) the Part 8 Claim Form

(b) this application

(c) the witness statement of Joe Bloggs (the Claimant's contractor) served herewith.

(Add Defendant's name and address)

DATED

Statement of Truth

*(I believe)(The Claimant believes) that the facts stated in this application are true.
*I am duly authorised by the Claimant to sign this statement.

Full name ---

Name of Claimant's solicitor's firm ---------------------------

Signed --

Position or office held ---

*(Claimant) (Litigation friend)(Claimant's solicitor) (if signing on behalf of firm or company)
**delete as appropriate*

Precedent for a claim for damages for breach of an Access Order

Application for damages regarding the breach of one or more terms or conditions of an Access Order made under the Access to Neighbouring Land Act 1992

(Same heading as claim form)

APPLICATION

This application is made by the Defendant pursuant to Section 6(2) of the Access to Neighbouring Land Act 1992.

The Defendant wishes to apply for an order that the Claimant pay him damages and that the costs of this application be assessed.

The Claimant has allowed his contractors to contravene the terms and conditions imposed in the Access Order made in this action on the 1st April 2001 by instructing them to work seven days a week to carry out the work specified in the Access Order. The Claimant's contractors have also been working on the servient land until 8.00 p.m. This is in breach of the Access Order which states that the work specified in the Access Order shall be carried out Monday to Friday from 8.00 am to 5.00 pm.

By reason of this breach the Defendant has suffered inconvenience and nuisance.

The Defendant will rely upon the following written evidence in support of this application: -

(a) his answer

(b) this application

(Add Claimant's name and address)

DATED

Statement of Truth

*(I believe)(The Defendant believes) that the facts stated in this application are true.
I am duly authorised by the Defendant to sign this statement.

Full name ---

Name of Defendant's solicitor's firm -------------------------

Signed ---

Position or office held ---------------------------------------

*(Defendant) (Litigation friend)(Defendant's solicitor) (if signing on behalf of firm or company)
delete as appropriate

Appendix 10

Selected extracts from relevant cases

ATKINSON v BETTISON [Plaint No. K. 737] COURT OF APPEAL [1955] 1 WLR

Landlord and Tenant - Act of 1954 - Business premises - Application for new tenancy - Landlord requiring possession for reconstruction - Reconstruction not primary purpose - "Substantial part" of premises a question of fact - Landlord and Tenant Act, 1954

Fact or Law. "Substantial."

The tenant of a provision shop applied to the landlord, a jeweller, for a new lease; the landlord refused, as he wished to open a jeweller's shop on the premises, which consisted of a shop on the ground floor and two storeys above used for storage.

On an application by the tenant to the County Court for an order under the Landlord and Tenant Act, 1954,[3] directing the grant of a new lease, the landlord, who could not oppose the application on the ground that he required possession for himself, as he had only recently

---

[3] Landlord and Tenant Act, 1954, s. 30: "(1) The grounds on which a landlord may oppose an application [for a new tenancy under the Act] ... are such of the following grounds as may be stated in the landlord's notice ... that is to say: - ... (1) that on the termination of the current tenancy the landlord intends to demolish or reconstruct the premises comprised in the holding or a substantial part of those premises or to carry out substantial work of construction on the holding or part thereof and that he could not reasonably do so without obtaining possession of the holding; (g) subject as hereinafter provided, that on the termination of the current tenancy the landlord intends to occupy the holding for the purposes, or partly for the purposes, of a business to be carried on by him therein, or as his residence. (2) The landlord shall not be entitled to oppose an application on the ground specified in paragraph (g) of the last foregoing subsection if the interest of the landlord ... was purchased or created after the beginning of the period of five years which ends with the termination of the current tenancy, ..."

acquired the premises, opposed on the ground that he required possession in order to reconstruct a substantial part of the premises to make them suitable for a jeweller's shop. The proposed work was the provision of a new shop-front of a different type, the demolition of a wall at the back of the shop, so as to throw the whole ground floor into the shop, a complete re-laying of the floor in a different material, and the provision of extensive new shop fittings. No work was to be done on the upper floors.

The County Court judge found that the real purpose of the landlord was to get possession so as to carry on a business of his own, and that the proposed reconstruction was merely ancillary to that purpose. He also found that the part of the premises affected was not a "substantial part," and directed the grant of a new lease. On an appeal by the landlord:

Held:

dismissing the appeal,

(1) that the landlord could not defeat the Act by putting forward an ancillary purpose open to him in law as if it were the main purpose;

(2) that the question whether the part of the premises affected was "substantial" was one of degree and therefore of fact; and, as there was evidence on which the judge could properly find that the part affected was not "substantial," the court could not disturb his finding.

BAKER v ELLISON
DIVISIONAL COURT [1914] 2 KB

Corporation - By-law - Wilful obstruction of corporation's servants in execution of their duty - Regulation prohibiting passengers riding on top of motor omnibuses on part of route - Refusal of passenger to descend from top - Delay of omnibus.

The E Corporation, who had statutory authority to run motor omnibuses, made a regulation prohibiting on one section of a particular route passengers riding on the top of the omnibuses. The regulation was made for the safety of passengers in view of the camber of the road, and notice thereof was exhibited on the top of the omnibuses, but attention was not drawn thereto on passengers' tickets. The appellant, who had previous knowledge of the regulation, was an outside passenger on an omnibus on the particular route and had paid the fare entitling him to travel over the section to which the regulation applied. When the omnibus reached the beginning of that section he refused to come down from the top although his attention was again called to the notice on the omnibus by the conductor and an inspector, the appellant stating that he had got his ticket and intended riding on the top to the terminus. The inspector declined to allow the omnibus to proceed while the appellant remained on the top, and it was thereby delayed twenty minutes. The appellant having been convicted of a breach of the corporation's by-law which provided that "No passenger or other person shall wilfully obstruct or impede any officer or servant of the council in the execution of his duty upon or in connection with any motor omnibus":

Held:

that the appellant was not entitled to be carried on the top of the omnibus on the part of the route to which the regulation applied inasmuch as the corporation had not, in respect of that part of the route, held themselves out as common carriers of passengers on the top of their omnibuses, or contracted to carry the appellant on the top of the omnibus; that the appellant's conduct amounted to wilful obstruction of the conductor and inspector within the meaning of the by-law; and, therefore, that the conviction was right.

BEWLAY (TOBACCONISTS) LTD v BRITISH BATA SHOE CO LTD [Plaint No. N 1690] COURT OF APPEAL [1959] 1 WLR

Landlord and Tenant - Business premises (security of tenure) - Landlord's intention to reconstruct - "Substantial part of premises" - Meaning - Totality of proposed work to be considered - Landlord and Tenant Act, 1954 (2 & 3 Eliz. 2, c. 56), s. 30 (1) (1).

Court of Appeal - County Court - Appeal from - Question of degree and fact.

Fact or Law - Landlord and tenant - Business premises - "Substantial part" question of fact - Landlord and Tenant Act, 1954, s. 30 (1) (f).

The landlords of a retail shop, who owned and occupied the adjoining shop, gave notice to the tenants determining the tenancy. On the tenants applying to the County Court under the Landlord and Tenant Act, 1954, for the grant of a new lease, the landlords opposed on the ground that on the termination of the tenancy they intended to demolish and reconstruct the premises or a substantial part thereof, and could not reasonably do so without obtaining possession. The scheme was to amalgamate the two self-contained shops into one shop. It was proved to the satisfaction of the judge that the landlords intended, *inter alia*[4], to reconstruct an entirely new shop front, involving the abolition of the existing means of access to the street, and to remove three-quarters of the dividing wall between the two shops, which necessitated alterations to some of the pillars supporting the ceiling. The judge considered that the proposed work involved both the demolition and reconstruction of a substantial part of the premises, and, accordingly, he refused the tenants' application. On appeal:

---

[4] among other things

Bewlay (Tobacconists) Ltd v British Bata Shoe Co Ltd [Plaint No. N 1690] Court of Appeal [1959] 1 WLR

Held:

dismissing the appeal, that there was evidence to support the judge's findings of fact, and that he had applied the correct test. He was entitled to look at the totality of the work which was proposed to be done in order to decide whether as a matter of fact and common sense those proposals came within the scope of paragraph (1) of Section 30 (1) of the Act of 1954.

BOMFORD (APPELLANT) v OSBORNE (INSPECTOR OF TAXES) (RESPONDENT) HOUSE OF LORDS [1942] AC

1941 Feb. 27, 28; Mar. 3; May 27. VISCOUNT SIMON LC, VISCOUNT MAUGHAM, LORD RUSSELL OF KILLOWEN, LORD WRIGHT, and LORD PORTER

Revenue - Income tax - Occupation of lands - Profits arising from lands occupied as .... gardens for the sale of the produce - Mixed farm - Divisibility - Practice - Form of special case stated by commissioners - Income Tax Act, 1918 (8 & 9 Geo. 5, c. 40), s. 149, sub-s. 1 (d); Sch. B, r. 8.

While a defined area which is not fenced round may be "gardens" for the purposes of r. 8 of Sch. B to the Income Tax Act, 1918, so long as it is a distinct and separate entity devoted to gardening, a field of farming land should not be called "gardens" merely because it grows products which used to be those characteristic of gardens, or even products which are still mainly or largely found in gardens. The main test whether lands are occupied as "gardens" within the meaning of the rule is that the defined area has some degree of fixity and local continuance and is subject to that kind and intensity of treatment which is characteristic of horticulture.

A single holding can be split into two parts with a view to applying r. 8 to one part of it while leaving the other part to be assessed under the ordinary provisions of Sch. B provided that the part which is "occupied as .... gardens for the sale of the produce" is distinct and separate from the other part. But (*per* Lord Maugham) *prima facie*[5] a

---

[5] on the face of it *or* as things seem at first

mixed farm is a single assessable unit and strong reasons must exist to justify dividing it for purposes of assessment.

Observations on the form of a special case stated by Commissioners of Income Tax.

Monro and Cobley v Bailey (1933) 102 LJ (KB) 471; 17 Tax Cas 607; and *Dennis v Hick* (1935) 19 Tax Cas 219, distinguished. *David Lowe & Sons, Ltd v Inland Revenue Commissioners* (1938) 21 Tax Cas 597 discussed.

Decision of the Court of Appeal reversed.

DUNNING v UNITED LIVERPOOL HOSPITALS' BOARD OF GOVERNORS [1972 D. No. 2591] COURT OF APPEAL [1973] 1 WLR

Practice - Discovery - Before commencement of proceedings - Disclosure of hospital case notes - Applicant's sudden collapse while being treated in hospital - Suspicion that mistake might have occurred - Medical adviser's opinion that disclosure of hospital records would allay suspicion - Whether applicant or hospital "likely to be a party to subsequent proceedings" - Effect of 10 years' delay - Administration of Justice Act 1970 (c.31), s. 31

In 1963 the applicant, a married woman who was then aged 56 and had had good health, developed a cough and was admitted to hospital for investigations. At first she seemed to improve but she suddenly became gravely ill and there appeared to be a change in her personality. The doctors were at first uncertain of the diagnosis and she was treated with different drugs. After 17 weeks she left hospital but her health was poor, her walking and memory were impaired and she had difficulty with housework. Her doctor said that her condition would improve but she said that it gradually deteriorated. In October 1969 she consulted solicitors and they obtained a report from a medical consultant. The report of May 11, 1970, said that assessment of the medical aspect of the matter had been considerably hampered by the absence of the clinical notes taken at the time of her original illness; it referred to the suspicions of the applicant's family that some mistake might have occurred when she was in hospital and concluded with the opinion that once the notes had been made available and their contents explained in lay terms the family's minds would be set at rest. The hospital refused to disclose the hospital case notes unless assured that no action would be brought.

In December 1970 the applicant was granted a legal aid certificate to take proceedings against the hospital. On July 1, 1971, an application for leave to bring such proceedings under the Limitation Act 1963 was adjourned without any order.

Dunning v United Liverpool Hospitals' Board of Governors [1972 D. No. 2591] Court of Appeal [1973] 1 WLR

By summons of May 12, 1971, application was made under Section 31 of the Administration of Justice Act 1970[6] for an order for the disclosure by the hospital of the medical records and case notes of the applicant's treatment from April to about September 1963. Caulfield J allowed the applicant's appeal from the order of the district registrar and ordered the hospital to produce the records and case notes to the applicant's medical adviser who had given the report of May 11, 1970.

On appeal by the hospital: -

Held:

dismissing the appeal (Stamp LJ dissenting), that, *per* Lord Denning MR, although the likelihood of the applicant commencing proceedings against the hospital depended on the outcome of the discovery sought, Section 31 of the Act of 1970 should not be construed so as to defeat one of its objects which was to enable a potential plaintiff to find out before commencing proceedings whether he had a reasonable cause of action (post, *p. 590E, h*), *per* James LJ, there was a reasonable prospect of the applicant commencing proceedings against the hospital (post, *pp. 59311-594A)* and that since the applicant had not been able to get any medical testimony to support her case until the section came into force on August 2, 1971, the order of the judge should in all the circumstances stand (post, *pp. 591 A, B, 594 A).*

---

[6]Administration of Justice Act 1970, s. 31: "On the application, in accordance with rules of court, of a person who appears to the High Court to be likely to be a party to subsequent proceedings in that court in which a claim in respect of personal injuries to a person or in respect of a person's death is likely to be made, the High Court shall, in such circumstances as may be specified in the rules, have power to order a person who appears to the court to be likely to be a party to the proceedings and to be likely to have or to have had in his possession, custody or power any documents which are relevant to an issue arising or likely to arise out of that claim - (a) to disclose whether those documents are in his possession, custody or power; and (b) to produce to the applicant such of those documents as are in his possession, custody or power."

Per Stamp LJ Section 31 of the Act of 1970 enables an order for discovery to be made when at the time the application comes before the court there are already grounds for thinking it "likely" that proceedings will be brought. "Likely" connotes that the respondent to the action is likely to be a party to a worthwhile action by a litigant not acting irresponsibly (post, *p. 591 D-F).*

Per Lord Denning MR The words "likely to be made," should be construed as meaning "may" or "may well be made" dependent on the outcome of the discovery (post, *p. 590E).*

Decision of Caulfield J affirmed.

English Clays Lovering Pochin & Co Ltd v Plymouth Corporation [1972 E. No. 1038] Court of Appeal [1974] 1 WLR

ENGLISH CLAYS LOVERING POCHIN & CO LTD v PLYMOUTH CORPORATION [1972 E. No. 1038] COURT OF APPEAL [1974] 1 WLR

Town Planning - Development, whether authorised - "Mineral undertakers" - Permission granted for winning and working of china clay in two separate areas connected by pipeline - Filtering and drying processes only of china clay in smaller area - Proposed development of smaller area -Whether part of "site" of "mining operations" - Whether "winning or working" clay - Whether smaller area "adjacent to" and belonging to "mine" - Town and Country Planning General Development Order 1963 (S.I. 1963 No. 709), arts. 2 (1), 3 (1), Sch. 1, Pt. I, Class XVIII

The plaintiff was a mineral undertaker of china clay in two areas of land. The larger area consisted of 1,500 acres from which china clay was taken from the ground. The smaller area of 80 acres was situated two miles away from the larger area but joined to it by a strip of land 25 feet wide along which ran a pipeline. A mixture of water and solid known as slurry was pumped through the pipe from the larger area to the smaller area, where it was processed to produce china clay in saleable form. The plaintiff wished to build a new plant and modernise existing buildings on the smaller area and contended that it was entitled to do so without planning permission, under article 3 of the Town and Country Planning General Development Order 1963, because the proposed buildings constituted development which the plaintiff as a mineral undertaker involved in the "winning or working" of china clay was entitled to effect on "land in or adjacent to and belonging to a quarry or mine" within Class XVIII (7) of Part I of Schedule 1 to the order. The defendant, the local planning authority, contended that planning permission was required.

The plaintiff applied by summons for a declaration that the development was permitted under article 3 of the order. Goulding J refused the declaration and dismissed the plaintiffs' summons on the grounds that, although the plaintiff was a mineral undertaker within article 2, the processes carried out on the smaller area were not part of the "winning or working" of the mineral and, although the smaller area was land belonging to a mine, in the context of planning, it was not "adjacent to" the larger area.

On appeal by the plaintiff: -

Held,

dismissing the appeal,

(1) that, since no clay in its natural form was to be found on the smaller area and no working or winning of clay took place there, the smaller area was not a mine within the definition of the order of 1963.

(2) that the three areas of land could not be described as "a site" on which mining operations were carried out; that "adjacent to" in the context of planning and in Class XVIII (2) of Schedule 1 to the order could not be construed as referring to land two miles away from a mine, albeit joined by a narrow strip of land, and, accordingly, article 3 of the order did not apply and the plaintiff required planning permission for the proposed buildings.

Fawcett Properties Ltd (Appellants) v Buckingham County Council (Respondents) House of Lords [1961] AC

FAWCETT PROPERTIES LTD (APPELLANTS) v BUCKINGHAM COUNTY COUNCIL (RESPONDENTS) HOUSE OF LORDS [1961] AC

LORD COHEN, LORD MORTON OF HENRYTON, LORD KEITH OF AVONHOLM, LORD DENNING and LORD JENKINS

Town and Country Planning - Development - Planning permission - Condition - Relation of condition to local planning considerations - Whether condition void for uncertainty - Town and Country Planning Act, 1947, ss. 14 (1), 36.

Housing - "Agricultural population" - Meaning - Housing Act, 1936, s. 115 (2)- Town and Country Planning Act, s. 119 (1). Statute - Construction - Uncertainty - Whether provision void - Provision incorporated in condition of planning permission - Whether condition valid.

By-law - Validity - Uncertainty - Condition of planning permission - Whether analogous to by-law - Town and Country Planning Act, 1947, ss. 14 (1), 36.

By Section 115 (2) of the Housing Act, 1936, which reproduces Section 34 (2) of the Housing Act, 1930, "agricultural population" is defined as "persons whose employment or latest employment is or was employment in agriculture or in an industry mainly dependent upon agriculture, and includes also the dependants of such persons as aforesaid."

By Section 14 of the Town and Country Planning Act, 1947: "(1) ... where application is made to the local planning authority for permission to develop land, that authority may grant permission either unconditionally or subject to such conditions as they think fit, or may refuse permission; and in dealing with any such application the local planning authority shall have regard to the provisions of the development plan, so far as material thereto, and to any other material considerations. (2) Without prejudice to the generality of the foregoing subsection, conditions may be imposed on the grant of permission to develop land thereunder - (a) for regulating the development or use of any land under the control of the applicant ..." By Section 36: "Where, under the foregoing provisions of this Part of this Act, a local planning authority are required to have regard to the provisions of the development plan in relation to the exercise of any of their functions, then, in relation to the exercise of those functions during any period before such a plan has become operative with respect to the area of that authority, that authority shall have regard to any directions which may be given to them by the Minister as to the provisions to be included in such a plan, and subject to any such directions shall have regard to the provisions which in their opinion will be required to be so included for securing the proper planning of the said area."

Section 119 (1) defined "agriculture" as including "horticulture, fruit growing, seed growing, dairy farming, the breeding and keeping of livestock (including any creature kept for the production of food, wool, skins or fur, or for the purpose of its use in the farming of land), the use of land as grazing land, meadow land, osier land, market gardens and nursery grounds, and the use of land for woodlands where that use is ancillary to the farming of land for other agricultural purposes."

In 1952 the respondent council, acting under the above sections, granted the appellants' predecessor in title permission to develop an area by building thereon a pair of cottages subject to a condition that: "The occupation of the houses shall be limited to persons whose employment or latest employment is or was employment in agriculture as defined by Section 119 (1) of the Town and Country Planning Act, 1947, or in forestry or in an industry mainly dependent upon agriculture and including also the dependants of such persons as aforesaid." The permission stated that the reason for imposing the condition was "because the council would not be prepared to permit the erection of dwelling-houses on this site unconnected with the use of the adjoining land for agricultural or similar purposes." The condition was registered as a local land charge. The property was within the metropolitan green belt, but there was no development plan yet in operation, although one was being prepared. At first the cottages were occupied by persons whose employment was within the terms of the condition, but the appellants, who acquired the freehold in 1956, sought a declaration that the condition was *ultra vires* the respondents, or was void for uncertainty, or was no longer effective, having been applicable only to the first occupants:

Held,

(1) that the imposition of a condition restricting the use of the premises according to the circumstances of the persons using them was not *ultra vires* the respondent council (post, *pp. 659, 675, 679, 684*).

(2) that the condition was not *ultra vires* in that it was not so wide that the result could not fairly and reasonably be said to relate to the permitted development or to any policy under the Act of 1947 (post, *pp. 660 to 662, 674, 678 to 680, 684 to 687*).

Dicta of Lord Greene MR in *Associated Provincial Picture Houses Ltd v Wednesbury Corporation* [1948] 1 KB 223, 233; 63 TLR 623; [1947] 2 All ER 680, CA, and of Lord Denning in *Pyx Granite Co Ltd v Ministry of Housing and Local Government* [1958] 1 QB 554, 572; [1958] 2 WLR 371; [1958] 1 All ER 625, CA applied.

(3) that the condition was not restricted to the first occupation of the cottages (post, *pp. 659, 675, 681, 684*).

(4) (Lord Morton of Henryton dissenting (post, *pp. 667 to 670*) that the condition was not void for uncertainty (post, *pp. 662, 663, 670 to 674, 676 to 678, 687 et seq.*).

The language of the definition of "agricultural population" in Section 34 (2) of the Housing Act, 1930, and Section 115 (2) of the Act of 1936, from which the language of the condition was substantially taken, has an intelligible and ascertainable content both in the Act and in the condition.

FRANKLIN v THE GRAMOPHONE COMPANY, LIMITED
COURT OF APPEAL [1948] 1 KB

1947 Dec. 8, 9, 10, 11, 12
SCOTT, SOMERVELL AND EVERSHED LJJ
1948 Feb. 4

Factory Acts - Regulations made under Acts - Dry grinder producing dust - Inhalation of dust by workman - Contraction of pneumoconiosis and tuberculosis - Death - Regulation providing for prevention of inhalation of dust Regulation exempting occupier of factory from liability - Supersession of section of Act by regulation - Common law duty of care for health of workmen - Liability of factory occupier at common law though requirements of regulation complied with - Factory and Workshop Act, 1901 (1 Edw. 7, c. 22), ss. 74, 79, 82 - Factories Act, 1937 s. 47, sub-s. 1 - s. 60, s. 159, sub-s. 1 - The Grinding of Metal (Miscellaneous Industries) Regulations, 1925 (St. R. & O. 1925, No. 904), exception IV, reg. 1.

The provisions of s. 47 of the Factories Act, 1937, have been superseded by the regulations in St. R. & O. 1925, No. 904 which were made under s. 79 of the Factory and Workshop Act, 1901, but were continued in force under s. 154 of the Act of 1937, and s. 47 now as no operation in a factory to which Order No. 904 applies.

The fact that the occupier of a factory has complied with all the requirements of regulations made under the Factory Acts which may be of limited scope, will not necessarily absolve him from liability for negligence at common law if he has not fulfilled his common law duty of care for the health of the workmen employed by him. Whether a factory owner is so relieved of his common law duty depends on the particular regulation in each case.

GRANADA THEATRES LTD v FREEHOLD INVESTMENTS (LEYTONSTONE) LTD CHANCERY DIVISION [1958] 1 WLR

Landlord and Tenant - Repairs - Covenant - "Structural repairs of a substantial nature" - Meaning of "structural repairs" - Meaning of "substantial."

By clause 2 (3) of a lease of a cinema the tenant covenanted to keep the demised premises

"in good and substantial repair and condition and properly decorated ... but nothing in this clause contained shall render the [tenants] liable for structural repairs of a substantial nature to the main walls roof foundations or main drains of the demised building."

By clause 3 (2) the landlords covenanted, except so far as the tenants were liable under their covenants, to

"repair maintain and keep the main structure walls roofs and drains of the demised premises in good structural repair and condition."

The roof being in disrepair and the cement rendering and brickwork of the front main elevation being defective, the tenants served a schedule of dilapidations on the landlords in respect of these, but the landlords did not execute the repairs. The tenants had the roof repaired themselves at a cost of £961, the work done including the repair of the front slated part. The landlords alleged that they had obtained a tender of £130 10s for the work, and that £961 was excessive. The tenants claimed damages for breach by the landlords of their covenant to repair the roof and a declaration that the landlords were liable to repair the front elevation:

Held:

(1) that "structural repairs" meant repairs to a structure.

(2) that the measure of the obligation to repair was the nature of the antecedent disrepair rather than the nature of the repair.

(3) that the roof and front wall were parts of the structure, so that repairs thereto would be "structural."

(4) that the antecedent disrepair was considerable, and accordingly "substantial," so that the necessary repairs were the responsibility of the landlords and not of the tenants.

Palser v Grinling [1948] AC 291; 64 TLR 2; [1948] 1 All ER 1 applied.

(5) that as the evidence as to the cost of effecting adequate repairs was unsatisfactory, there must be an inquiry as to damages.

GREEN v MOORE
DIVISIONAL COURT [1982] QB

Police - Obstruction - Warning to prevent commission of offence - Police anticipating breach of licensing laws by publican - Publican warned of police investigation - No offence committed - Whether warning obstruction of police in execution of duty - Police Act 1964 (c. 48), s. 51 (3) (as amended by Criminal Law Act 1977 (c. 45), s. 31 (1), Sch. 6)

The landlord of licensed premises was suspected of selling or supplying intoxicating liquor outside permitted hours, contrary to Section 59 of the Licensing Act 1964. One evening within the permitted hours, the defendant warned him that police officers, suspecting that an offence would be committed that evening, intended to raid the premises. A police officer in plain clothes was in the public bar and other officers were in the vicinity waiting until the permitted hours had expired. After the defendant's warning, the staff and customers in the public bar began to treat the plain clothes officer, who was a stranger, in a markedly unfriendly manner. There was no contravention of the permitted hours or any other provision of the Licensing Act 1964 that evening. The defendant was charged with wilfully obstructing police officers in the execution of their duty, contrary to Section 51 (3) of the Police Act 1964. He was convicted by justices and appealed to the Crown Court. At the close of the prosecution case, the court accepted the defendant's submission that the prosecution had failed to prove that at the time of the alleged obstruction the person assisted by it was committing or had committed an offence and allowed the appeal.

On the prosecutor's appeal:

Held,

allowing the appeal, that in considering a charge of obstruction under Section 51 (3) the court had to ask itself whether there was any obstruction of a constable; whether the constable was acting in the execution of his duty; and whether the obstruction was intended to obstruct the constable; that since there was no real distinction between a warning given in order to suspend the commission of an offence whilst there was a danger of detection and a warning given in order to postpone the commission of an offence until after the danger of detection had passed, the offence was not limited to an obstruction of a constable where a crime was being committed or had been committed, and that, accordingly, since the police were acting in the execution of their duty in investigating an expected crime and were deprived by the defendant's warning of the opportunity of seeing whether in normal circumstances the permitted hours would be observed, the case would be remitted to the Crown Court to continue the hearing (post, *pp. 1051G-H, 1052A-F*).

Harris v Birkenhead Corporation & Another
Pascoe and Another Third Party
Alliance Assurance Co Ltd Fourth Party
[1970 H. No. 278] Court of Appeal 1 WLR

HARRIS v BIRKENHEAD CORPORATION & ANOTHER PASCOE AND ANOTHER THIRD PARTY ALLIANCE ASSURANCE CO LTD FOURTH PARTY [1970 H. No. 278] COURT OF APPEAL 1 WLR

Occupiers' Liability - Occupation - Compulsory Purchase Order - Local authority serving notice to treat and notice of entry on owner of house - House vacated and damaged by vandals - Child trespasser injured - Whether local authority or owner in occupation - Right of control - Whether local authority having knowledge of danger - Occupiers' Liability Act 1957 s. 2

A corporation had a programme of slum clearance and, between compulsory acquisition of properties and their demolition prior to building new houses, it was their practice to brick up all ground floor openings and cut off the water supply to prevent the properties from being damaged by mischievous children and vandals. In furtherance of that slum clearance programme, the corporation made a Compulsory Purchase Order for an area which included a house owned by the second defendant, managed for her by estate agents and occupied by an excellent tenant. On July 31, 1967, the corporation served on the second defendant a notice to treat and a notice of entry. A notice of entry was also served on the tenant. It stated that the corporation would enter the property 14 days from the date of service but it was accompanied by a letter which stated that the corporation required vacant possession and would offer the tenant accommodation. The tenant informed both the corporation and the estate agents that she would make her own arrangements and would soon move. She moved from the house by December 23 and, at that time, the property was in good condition.

By March 6, 1968, when the plaintiff, aged 4, wandered from a playground into the house, the corporation had not bricked it up and vandals had broken down the front door and done considerable damage including removing the glass from a second floor window. The plaintiff fell 30 feet from that window with the result that she suffered severe brain damage. She brought an action for damages against the corporation and the second defendant claiming that they were in breach of the duty owed to her under the Occupiers' Liability Act 1957. The judge held that the corporation, and not the second defendant, was the occupier for the purpose of the Act and, since the corporation knew of the likelihood of empty property in the area being damaged and children playing there and the plaintiff's action was one that a humane person exercising common sense could have expected or prevented, the corporation was liable for the injuries she received.

On appeal by the corporation: -

Held,

dismissing the appeal, (1) that, since the corporation by the notice to treat was asserting its right to enter and control the property after the expiration of 14 days and had continued to assert that right at any time it considered fit, the corporation, having the immediate right of control, became the occupier of the property as soon as it ceased to be physically occupied by the tenant (post, *pp. 287E-F, 291C, 292B-C*)

Dictum of Lord Denning in *Wheat v E. Lacon & Co Ltd* [1966] AC 552, 578, HL(E) applied.

Per Megaw LJ There was no duty owed to the corporation by the owner or the tenant of the house to give the corporation notice that they were leaving the house empty for the corporation to enter and control the property (post, *p. 287F-G*).

(2) That the circumstances were such that if the corporation, as occupier, had known that the house was empty, it was under a duty to protect the infant plaintiff from the danger of trespassing in the property; that, since the tenant had informed an officer of the corporation that at some time she would be moving from the house and other officers, having the duty to secure empty houses in the clearance area against vandals, must have observed that the house was empty, the corporation ought to have known that the house was empty and, accordingly, it had the requisite knowledge to make it liable to the plaintiff for the injuries she had received (post, *pp. 289D-F, 290F - 291A, H – 292B*).

In re HATCHEK'S PATENTS
Ex parte ZERENNER
CHANCERY DIVISION [1909] 2 Ch

1909 March 3, 4, 26
PARKER J

Patent - Revocation - Patented Article or Process manufactured or carried on exclusively or mainly out of United Kingdom - Patents and Designs Act, 1907 ss. 24, 27.

Sect. 24 of the Patents and Designs Act, 1907, deals primarily with cases where the trade of this country has been injured by an abuse of the monopoly conferred by the patent, irrespective of anything which is being done abroad, while s. 27 deals primarily with cases where the object or effect of the use of such rights in the way they have been used has been to favour the development of industries abroad at the expense of industries in the United Kingdom.

The keynote of s. 27 is forfeiture of the patent for the abuse of the monopoly at the instance of a common informer, and any one, whether a foreign or a British subject, and whatever his motive, can, by satisfying the Comptroller of the existence of the circumstances contemplated in sub-s. 1, throw on the patentee the onus of proving, to prevent revocation, that the patented process or article is carried on or manufactured to an adequate extent within the United Kingdom, or of giving a satisfactory reason why it is not so carried on or manufactured.

Sect. 27 does not mean that in every case where more than 50 per cent. of the patented articles manufactured anywhere are made abroad the patentee can be called upon to defend his patent rights; if the article is manufactured in the United Kingdom to as great an extent as can reasonably be expected, having regard to the industrial development of other countries, no presumption against the patentee arises.

Sect. 27, sub-s. 1, institutes a comparison between the extent to which the article or process is manufactured or carried on in this country and the extent to which it is manufactured or carried on abroad, whether the articles are or are not imported into this country, and the section is meant to hit every abuse of the patentee's monopoly the object or result of which is to benefit foreigners at the expense of traders within the United Kingdom.

In determining whether there has been "adequate" manufacturing in the United Kingdom, or whether "satisfactory reasons" for the inadequacy are given by the patentee, it is left to the Comptroller, subject to appeal to the court, to determine in each case, and having regard to all the circumstances, whether the home manufacture is adequate, or, if not, whether the reasons are satisfactory, he bearing in mind (a) that that manufacture is not adequate if it is lessened by the patentee exercising his patent rights to the hurt of British industry - e.g., by giving foreign traders a preference as to licences or otherwise over British traders - and (b) that reasons are not satisfactory which do not account for the inadequacy of the home manufacture by causes operating irrespective of any abuse of the monopoly.

On the other hand, a patentee who has allowed part of the demand in this country to be supplied by the importation of goods from abroad has not necessarily precluded himself from proving that there is adequate home manufacture or giving satisfactory reasons for the inadequacy of that manufacture, the policy of s. 27 being to secure fair play between foreign and British industries.

Statement of matters which may be considered in determining whether home manufacture is adequate, and what are satisfactory reasons for the inadequacy of that manufacture.

Sect. 27 applies both to patents in existence before the Act of 1907 and patents subsequently granted, although reasons might be accepted as satisfactory in the case of the former which would not be so accepted in the latter; but the fact that a patentee has before the Act precluded himself by licence or contract from working his patent in this country is not a satisfactory reason.

Observations on the then existing rules of procedure as to applications for the revocation of patents.

In 1900 two patents were granted to H. for inventions relating to a process of manufacturing imitation stone slabs. The invention was in commercial operation in Germany, France, and Belgium, but was never worked in the United Kingdom. The patentee devoted himself to the establishment abroad of industries in which the patented process was carried on, and used his monopoly to secure to a Belgian company, to whom in 1905 he granted an exclusive licence for the United Kingdom, the monopoly of selling in the United Kingdom articles manufactured by the company in Belgium:

Held:

affirming the Comptroller's decision, that the patent ought to be revoked forthwith, although in July, 1908, the patentee and the Belgian company had issued newspaper advertisements in the United Kingdom expressing their willingness to sell or enter into working arrangements for the manufacture of goods in the United Kingdom under the patented process.

HILLINGDON LONDON BOROUGH COUNCIL v CUTLER COURT OF APPEAL [1968] 1 QB

HARMAN, DAVIES and RUSSELL LJJ

Housing - Unfit for human habitation - Demolition Order – "Forthwith" - Dispute whether original Demolition Orders valid - Fresh Demolition Orders served more than six months after service of "time and place" notices - Whether fresh Demolition Orders made "forthwith" - No appeal by owner against orders -Whether debarred from asserting their invalidity - Demolition work carried out by contractor under lump sum contract - Contractor given right to retain materials recovered from demolished dwellings - Notional credit given for value of materials - Whether proper procedure for execution of work - Housing Act, 1957 ss. 16 (1), 17 (1), 2 0 (1), 2 3 (1) (2), 3 7 (1).

A local authority, being satisfied that certain dwellings were unfit for human habitation and could not be rendered so fit at reasonable expense, served "time and place" notices on May 5, 1961, pursuant to Section 16 (1) of the Housing Act, 1957,[7] on which he may wish to

[7] Housing Act, 1957, s. 16: "Where a local authority, on the consideration of an official representation, or a report from any of their officers, or other information in their possession, are satisfied that any house – *(a)* is unfit for human habitation, and *(b)* is not capable at a reasonable expense of being rendered so fit, they shall serve upon the person having control of the house, … notice of the time (being some time not less than 21 days after the service of the notice) and place at which the condition of the house and any offer with respect to the carrying out of works, or the future user of the house, which he may wish to submit will be considered by them. (2) Every person upon whom such a notice is served under subs. (1) of this section shall be entitled to be heard when the matter is so taken into consideration. ..." the owner, appointing May 31, 1961, as the time when the appropriate committee of the local authority would consider the condition of the dwellings and any offers which the owner might wish to make with respect to the carrying out of works. The owner duly attended the meeting of the appropriate committee and made no objection to their demolition. On June 27, 1961, the local authority served Demolition Orders on the owner. He alleged that they were not duly signed by the town clerk, as required by the Act of 1957, and were, therefore, invalid. The local authority asserted that they were so signed and asked the owner to send them

submit will be considered by them. (2) Every person upon whom such a notice is served under subs. (1) of this section shall be entitled to be heard when the matter is so taken into consideration. ..."

S.17: "(1) If no such undertaking as is mentioned in the last foregoing section is accepted by the local authority ... then, subject to the provisions of this section, the local authority shall forthwith make a Demolition Order for the demolition of the premises to which the notice given under the last foregoing section relates. ..."

S. 20: "Any person aggrieved by - (a) a demolition or closing order made under this part of this Act, may, within 21 days after the date of the service of the order or notice, appeal to the County Court within the jurisdiction of which the premises to which the order or notice relates are situate, and no proceedings shall be taken by the local authority to enforce any order or notice in relation to which an appeal is brought before the appeal has been finally determined. ..."

S. 23: "(1) Subject to the provisions of this part of this Act, when a Demolition Order under this part of this Act has become operative, the owner or owners of the premises to which it applies shall demolish those premises within the time limited in that behalf by the order; and if the premises are not demolished within that time, the local authority shall enter and demolish the premises and sell the materials thereof. (2)

---

back, so that they could see whether the town clerk's signature appeared on them. The owner said that he sent them back, but the local authority claimed that they never received them. In order to resolve the controversy the local authority served fresh Demolition Orders on January 26, 1962, on the owner. The owner not having complied with those orders, the local authority had the demolition work carried out by a demolition contractor who quoted a lump sum price for the job on the basis that he could retain the materials recovered from the demolished dwellings. The contract with the contractor thus provided for the net cost of demolition. The public health inspector who entered into the contract on behalf of the authority had worked out in his mind the gross cost of demolition and the value of materials to be recovered and was satisfied that the lump sum price quoted by the contractor was reasonable.

Any expenses incurred by an authority under the foregoing subsection, after giving credit for any amount realised by the sale of materials, may be recovered by them as a simple contract debt from the owner of the premises. ..."

S. 37: "(1) Any notice, demand or order against which an appeal might be brought to a County Court under this Part of this Act shall, if no such appeal is brought, become operative on the expiration of 21 days from the date of the service of the notice, demand or order, and shall be final and conclusive as to any matters which could have been raised on such an appeal. ..."

On a claim by the local authority to recover the expense of demolition against the owner as a contract debt under Section 23 (2) of the Act of 1957, the owner contended that the Demolition Orders served in January, 1962, were invalid because they had not been made "forthwith" within Section 17 (1), alternatively that the sum claimed was not "... expenses incurred ... after giving credit for the amount realised by the sale of materials" within Section 23 (2) because there had been no sale of the materials. The judge held that the demolition orders were valid and that there had been sufficient compliance by the authority with Section 23 (2). He, accordingly, gave judgement for the local authority. On appeal by the owner:-

Held:

dismissing the appeal,

(1) that even if the Demolition Orders had not been made "forthwith" within the meaning of Section 17 (1) of the Housing Act, 1957, that would not have invalidated the orders in the absence of any detriment to the owner, but that, in any event, "forthwith" only meant within a reasonable time thereafter, and in the circumstances of the present case, the Demolition Orders served in January, 1962, had been made within a reasonable time of the "time and place" notices served under Section 16 (1) in May, 1961, and were

accordingly valid orders. *Brown v Bonnyrigg Magistrates, 1936 S.C. 258* applied.

In *re Southam. ex parte Lamb (1881) 19 Ch.D. 169, C.A.* considered.

(2) that the making of a lump sum contract with a demolition contractor under which there was, as in the present case, a notional credit for the value of the materials recovered from the demolished premises, so that the owner was only charged the net cost of demolition, was a sufficient compliance with the requirement in Section 23 (2) on a local authority to give credit for any amount realised by the sale of materials, and, accordingly, the local authority's claim succeeded .

Per Davies and Russell L.JJ.: In any event, the owner probably could not allege that the Demolition Orders were invalid because not having appealed against them under Section 20 (1) he was debarred by Section 37 (1) from asserting their invalidity .

HINCHLIFFE v SHELDON
QUEEN'S BENCH DIVISION [1955] 1 WLR

LORD GODDARD CJ, CASSELS AND STREATFEILD JJ

Licensing - Police right to enter licensed premises - Obstruction - Attempted entry by police - Warning given to licensee by third party - Police detained from entering - Whether obstruction of police in execution of duty - Prevention of Crimes Amendment Act, 1885 (48 & 49 Vict. c. 75), s. 2 - Licensing Act, 1953 (1 & 2 Eliz. 2, c. 46), s. 151 (1).

Criminal Law - Police obstruction.

H., the son of the licensee of a hotel, returned to the hotel one night after permitted licensing hours and, seeing that police were watching the premises, knocked at the door and shouted warnings to his parents that the police were about. A police constable immediately knocked at the door, but some ten minutes elapsed before the licensee admitted him to the premises. No licensing offence was proven against the licensee, but H. was charged with obstructing the police in the execution of their duty, contrary to Section 2 of the Prevention of Crimes Amendment Act, 1885, and convicted:

Held:

that the police had a right, under Section 151 of the Licensing Act, 1953, to enter licensed premises at any time to see whether or not offences were being committed, and to detain them from so doing, as H. had done by giving a warning, obviously amounted to obstruction of the police in the execution of their duty and, therefore, justices were entitled to convict H.

Bastable v Little [1907] 1 KB 59; 23 T.L.R. 38 and *Betts v Stevens* [1910]1 KB 1; 26 T.L.R. 5 distinguished

Ex parte Lamb *In re* Southam
Court of Appeal 19 ChD

Ex parte LAMB *In re* SOUTHAM
COURT OF APPEAL 19 ChD

Appeal - Time - Notice to Registrar of County Court - "Forthwith" - Bankruptcy Rules, 1870, rr. 143, 144.

When an act is required by a statute or a rule of court to be done "forthwith," the word "forthwith" must be construed with regard to the object of the provision and the circumstances of the case.

The London agents of the country solicitors of an appellant from an order made by a County Court in bankruptcy entered the appeal with the Registrar of Appeals in London on Friday, the 5th of August, the last possible day, but did not post a copy of the appeal notice to the country solicitors until the following day, and it was not received by them until Monday, the 8th of August, and on that day they sent a copy of the notice to the Registrar of the County Court:

Held:

that the copy of the notice had not been sent to the Registrar of the County Court "forthwith" on entering the appeal as required by rule 144, and that consequently the appeal was out of time.

JACKSON (RESPONDENT) v HALL AND ANOTHER(APPELLANTS) WILLIAMSON (APPELLANT) v THOMPSON AND ANOTHER (RESPONDENTS) HOUSE OF LORDS [1980] AC

Agricultural Holding - Death of tenant - Succession to tenancy - "Eligible person" - Applicant occupier of other agricultural land at time of tenant's death - Interest therein assigned by time of application - Whether "eligible person" - Material time for determining eligibility - Joint occupier of commercial unit - Whether "the occupier" - Agriculture (Miscellaneous Provisions) Act 1976 (c. 55), ss. 1 s (2) (c), 20 (1)

Statute - Construction - Statutory instrument as aid - Statutory instrument made in exercise of power contained in Act - Whether to be relied on as aid to construction of Act

By Section 20 of the Agriculture (Miscellaneous Provisions) Act 1976, an "eligible person" may apply for a tenancy of an agricultural holding, and by Section 18 (2):

" 'eligible person' means ... a survivor of the deceased [tenant] in whose case the following conditions are satisfied ... (c) he is not the occupier of a commercial unit of agricultural land within the meaning of Part 11 of the Agriculture Act 1967 ..."

In *Jackson v Hall* a partnership consisting of a father and two sons farmed two adjacent farms. One farm was owned by the respondent landlords and let to the father. The other farm, which was a commercial unit of agricultural land within the meaning of Part II of the Act of 1967, was owned by the father and let to the partnership. Following the death of the father, one of the sons assigned his interest in the father's farm to his brother and made an application under Section 20 (1) of the Act of 1976 for a direction entitling him to a tenancy of the tenanted farm. The agricultural land tribunal held that he was not an "eligible person" within Section 18 (2) of the Act because he had not satisfied the condition in paragraph (c) at the date of his father's death. On a special case stated by the tribunal, Sir Douglas Frank Q.C., sitting as a deputy judge of the Queen's Bench Division, upheld the tribunal's decision, but the Court of Appeal by a majority (Brandon LJ dissenting) allowed an appeal by the applicant holding that the material times for satisfying the requirement of being an "eligible person" as defined in Section 18 (2) were the dates of the application and the hearing before the tribunal and that it had not been necessary for the applicant to satisfy the condition in paragraph (c) at the date of his father's death. The landlords appealed.

In *Williamson v Thompson* the deceased father had been the tenant of "riverside land," which was part of an agricultural unit farmed by his two sons. The agricultural unit excluding the riverside land, was a commercial unit within the meaning of Part II of the Act of 1967. The father died, and the applicant, one of the sons, applied under Section 20 (1) of the Act of 1976 for a direction entitling him to a tenancy of the riverside land. The agricultural land tribunal held that he was eligible to do so. Michael Kempster Q.C., sitting as a deputy judge of the Queen's Bench Division, allowed an appeal by the landlords, holding that a joint occupier of a commercial unit was "the occupier" for the purposes of Section 18 (2) (c) of the Act of 1976. He gave the applicant leave to appeal directly from his judgement to the House of Lords. The applicant appealed.

The appeals were heard together in the House of Lords and on the hearing the applicant in *Jackson v Hall* was given leave to argue the point, which he had not argued below, that joint, as opposed to sole, occupation of a commercial unit of agricultural land was not a bar to eligibility under Section 18 (2) (c) of the Act of 1976: -

Held:

allowing the appeal in *Jackson v Hall* and dismissing the appeal (Lord Russell of Killowen dissenting) in *Williamson v Thompson*

(1) that on the true construction of Section 18 of the Agriculture (Miscellaneous Provisions) Act 1976 eligibility for succession to a deceased tenant's tenancy had to exist at the date of the tenant's death and an applicant was precluded from being an eligible person by Section 18 (2) (c) if at that date he was the occupier of a commercial unit of agricultural land within the meaning of that paragraph, and he could not subsequently become an eligible person by thereafter divesting himself of his occupation (post, *pp. 884B-C, 886A-B, 89 (C, 892A, 891G – 894B, 896B*).

Per curiam. The applicant must also be eligible at the date of the application and at the date of the hearing before the tribunal (post, *pp. 884C, 886A-B, 891E -F, 896B*).

Per Lord Russell of Killowen. I would not suppose that a precipitately remarrying wife would thereby lose her eligibility under Section 18 (1) (a) (post, *p. 893B-C*).

(2) (Lord Russell of Killowen dissenting) that on the true construction of Section 18 (2) (c) "the occupier" included a joint occupier (post, *pp. 885F, 886A-B, 887F-H, 896B*).

Per curiam. Rules made in the exercise of a statutory power, at least where not affirmatively approved by Parliament, cannot be relied on as an aid to the construction of the statute (post, *pp. 884G-H, 886A-B, 889F, 896B*).

Jones v Scullard
Queen's Bench Division [1898] 2 QB

JONES v SCULLARD.
QUEEN'S BENCH DIVISION [1898] 2 QB

1898 April 29; Aug. 9
LORD RUSSELL of KILLOWEN CJ

Master and Servant - Servant of one Person hired by another to Drive his Carriage - Liability of Hirer for Negligence of Driver.

The defendant was the owner of a brougham, horses, and harness which he kept at a livery-stable. The keeper of the livery-stable was in the habit of supplying the defendant with one of his own servants to drive the brougham. One day, whilst the brougham was being driven with one of the defendant's horses, the driver, owing to his negligence, as the jury found, lost control of the horse, which dashed through the window of the plaintiffs shop and did damage. The man who was driving the brougham at the time of the accident had continuously driven the defendant for the preceding six weeks, and at the time of the accident was wearing a suit of livery which had been supplied to him by the defendant.

Held,

that upon these facts there was evidence on which a jury might find that the driver at the time of the accident was acting as the servant of the defendant, so as to render the defendant responsible for the consequences of his negligence.

METHUEN-CAMPBELL v WALTERS
COURT OF APPEAL [1978] 247 EG 899

June 21 1978

Leasehold Reform Act 1967 - Whether paddock forms part of "premises" for purposes of enfranchisement - Whether an "appurtenance" - Whether within the "curtilage" of the house - Meaning of "curtilage" - Paddock not an "appurtenance" nor part of the "curtilage"

This was an appeal by Christopher Paul Manser Methuen-Campbell, of Penrice Castle, Reynoldston, Swansea, against an order of Deputy Judge Evans at Swansea County Court on August 19 1977, whereby he declared that, for the purposes of the Leasehold Reform Act 1967, the premises in respect of which the tenant, Kate Evelyn Walters, qualified for enfranchisement, included a paddock to the south-west of the house. The paddock was demised to the tenant and was separated from the garden by a gate.

Jules Sher (instructed by Dawson & Co) appeared for the appellant; Ian Edwards Jones QC and Trevor Davies (instructed by L C Thomas & Son, of Neath) represented the respondent.

Giving the first judgement at the invitation of Buckley LJ, GOFF LJ said that the appellant had become entitled as trustee to the freehold reversion immediately expectant on the termination of a lease for a term of 99 years the residue of which was vested in the respondent. The lease, which was dated August 27 1894, demised the house and premises including the paddock. The area of the house and garden was some 0.5 acre, and that of the paddock was some 1.6 acres. The respondent had sought a conveyance of the freehold, and the question was whether she was entitled to a conveyance of the whole of the demised premises, or whether the appellant was entitled to exclude the paddock.

At the trial it was considered that the question turned solely on the definition of "premises" in Section 2(3) of the Leasehold Reform Act

1967, in which, it was contended, the only relevant words were "garden" and "appurtenances." The learned deputy judge held that the paddock was not a "garden" but was an "appurtenance." He dismissed the appellant's application for a declaration that the house and premises which the respondent was entitled to have conveyed to her did not include the paddock, and made a counter-declaration sought by the respondent that the whole of the paddock was included.

The appellant contended that the learned deputy judge was wrong, firstly because (1) a paddock as a matter of law could not be an appurtenance to a house, since only an incorporeal hereditament could be an appurtenance to land; (2) if that were wrong, the paddock here did not satisfy the proper test for an appurtenance; (3) the conditions as to user in Section 2(3) of the Act were not satisfied at the relevant time.

The respondent disputed all those contentions, but, in addition, by a respondent's notice, prayed that the paddock was within Section 2(3) and, by an amendment which the court had allowed, contended further, that the paddock, if not an appurtenance, or part of the garden, was within a "house" as that word was used in Part I of the Act.

As to whether land could be appurtenant to land, the present position seemed to his Lordship to be that stated by Slesser LJ in *Trim v Sturminster RDC* [1938] 2 KB 508, at p 515: "It is now beyond question that, broadly speaking, nothing will pass under a demise by the word `appurtenances' which would not equally pass under a conveyance of the principal subject matter without addition of that word. That is to say, as pointed out in the earlier case of *Bryan v Wetherhead* (1625) 1 Cro Car 17, that the word 'appurtenances' will pass with the house, the orchard, yard, curtilage and garden, but not the land."

Mr Edwards-Jones argued that the present legal meaning was wider, and was the same as the popular meaning foreshadowed as long ago as the third year of William and Mary. He contended that the legal meaning comprehended anything used and occupied with or for the benefit of the house, whether as a matter of convenience or as an amenity. He further contended that even if that was not the meaning (and his Lordship thought it was not) there was here a context which would give the word a wider meaning. He relied on the fact that "appurtenance" in Section 2(3) followed the words "garage, outhouse, garden, yard." The definition included the words "let to him with the house and occupied and used for the purposes of the house . . ." and Mr Edwards-Jones rightly pointed out that though one might enjoy a right to light one certainly could never occupy it. He further pointed out that incorporeal hereditaments were exclusively dealt with by Section 10.

If indeed a context were needed to enable "appurtenances" to include corporeal as well as incorporeal hereditaments, his Lordship would agree, but he saw nothing in the context to enlarge the meaning of the word beyond the curtilage of the house. Mr Edwards-Jones further contended that on the facts of the case, the paddock was in any event within the "curtilage." He relied on the fact that the house, garden and premises were all let as one entire unit, but that of itself was not, his Lordship thought, relevant; certainly not of much weight. Mr. Edwards-Jones relied also on evidence of Oakley Walters FRICS that the land was vital to the enjoyment of the house, and that the house and field were one unit, and on evidence of Hugh Rees FRICS that the paddock was an essential element in the use of this type of house, and that any purchaser would expect some land with it. The evidence, however, went no further than to show that the paddock was a valuable amenity; that did not make it an "appurtenance" or bring it within the "curtilage" of the house.

He further submitted that the paddock was part of the residential unit, and the court ought to take a commonsense view of the word "appurtenance," or of the definition of "house and premises" as a whole, and treat the paddock as part of the house itself, or being within the word "garden." But the Act was not dealing with residential units; it was one to give people whose houses were held on long leases at a low rent security of tenure in their homes, and it specified what was meant by "house and premises." His Lordship was not able to adopt Mr. Edwards-Jones' wide construction of the section, bearing in mind that this was a section giving the tenant a compulsory right to purchase, and was therefore expropriatory. Mr. Edwards-Jones relied on cases under Section 92 of the Lands Clauses Consolidation Act 1845, including *Barnes v Southsea Railway Co* (1884) 27 Ch D 536 and *St Thomas's*

Hospital Governors v Charing Cross Railway Co (1861) 30 LJCh 395. But the 1967 Act was an expropriation Act, and in those cases the court was considering the protection of land from undue expropriation, and his Lordship did not think they helped very much.

In his Lordship's view it was impossible to treat the paddock as part of the house simpliciter[8], but only if it was an appurtenance. Likewise it could not be regarded as part of the garden. The garden was not part of the house, and it would be extraordinary if the paddock, separated from the house, could be regarded as part of the house.

In the end, his Lordship thought, the crux of the problem was whether the paddock was within "the curtilage." The word "curtilage", *prima facie*, was of narrow import. The *Oxford English Dictionary* defined it as a "small courtyard or piece of ground attached to a dwelling-house and forming one enclosure with it," but a note in *Stroud's Judicial Dictionary* suggested that it might be wider than that. Their Lordships had looked at some of the cases cited in *Stroud,* but he (his Lordship) did not think they afforded any assistance.

It was a question of fact in each case, and he could not find that that comparatively extensive piece of pasture ought to be so regarded, particularly where, as here, it was clearly divided off physically from the house right from the start, and certainly at all material times.

The 1967 Act did not necessarily give the tenant in each case the right to everything contained in his demise: see *per* Upjohn LJ (as he then was) in *Clymo (Valuation Officer) v Shell Mex & BP Ltd* (1963) 10 RRC 85, at p 98, where he quoted with approval the passage cited above by Slesser LJ in *Trim's* case.

The paddock was not, in his Lordship's judgement, an "appurtenance."

---

[8] Simply or absolutely, summarily

MILLER v OWNERS OF THE SHIP OTTILIE COURT OF APPEAL [1944]1 KB

Workmen's compensation - Fisherman - "Remunerated ... mainly by shares in the profits" - Poundage exceeding wages, risk money, and value of food - Workmen's Compensation Act (15 & 16 Geo. S, c. 84), s. 35, sub-s. 2.

The workman, who was employed as cook on a steam fishing-trawler belonging to the employers, was paid weekly a basic wage of *£21. 3s 9d.,* and he also received *£11. 5s 0d.* risk money, and food valued at *18s,* a total of *£41. 6s 9d.* In addition he was entitled to "poundage" based on profits which amounted in his case to £7. *9s 0d.* a week:

Held: that the workman was "remunerated .... mainly by shares in the profits .... of the working of the vessel" within the meaning of s. 35, sub-s. 2 of the Workmen's Compensation Act, 1925, and that the Act did not apply to him.

Mills & Rockleys Limited v Leicester City Council
King's Bench Division [1946] 1 KB

MILLS & ROCKLEYS LIMITED v LEICESTER CITY COUNCIL
KING'S BENCH DIVISION [1946] 1 KB

Local government - Planning scheme - Interim Development Order - Prohibition of use of wall of house for advertising - Validity - Town and Country Planning Act, 1932 (22 & 23 Geo. 5, c. 48), s. 47 - Town and Country Planning (Interim Development) Act, 1943 (6 & 7 Geo. 6, c. 29), s. 5.

The Town and Country Planning Act, 1932, is wide enough to enable a local authority, in preparing a scheme under that Act, to protect a part or the whole of their district with regard to advertisements and under s. 47 of that Act the local authority may then require to be taken down or may otherwise deal with advertisements which have been put up and are unsightly or unsuitable. But by s. 47, sub-s. 8, of that Act a scheme is not to contain any provision prohibiting or controlling the erection or use of structures for the purpose of advertising and that provision is not affected by anything in the Town and Country Planning (Interim Development) Act, 1943.

Where, therefore, the owners of a house in an area in respect of which a scheme was in course of preparation painted an exterior wall of the house with a view to its use for the display of advertisements and the local authority in pursuance of s. 5 of the Act of 1943, served on them a notice that such use was prohibited on the ground that it was a development contrary to an Interim Development Order made by them:

Held:

that the order was bad and must be set aside.

In re MUSCOVITCH Ex parte MUSCOVITCH
COURT OF APPEAL [1939] Ch

Bankruptcy - Appeal - Notice to registrar - Time - "Forthwith" - Bankruptcy Act, 1914 (4 & 5 Geo. 5, c. 59), s. 109, sub-s. 4; s. 147, sub-s. 1 - Bankruptcy Rules, 1915, rr. 132, 385, 386.

Rule 132 of the Bankruptcy Rules, 1915, provides that: "Upon entering an appeal, a copy of the notice of appeal shall forthwith be sent by the appellant to the registrar of the court appealed from, who shall mark thereon the date when received and forthwith file the same with the proceedings."

On October 21, 1938, an order was made by the County Court of Cardiff and Barry, under which the appellants' discharge from bankruptcy was suspended for six months. The appellants entered an appeal on October 25. The appellants sent a copy of the notice of appeal in time to be effected on October 28 in Cardiff:

Held:

(affirming the decision of the Divisional Court), that the copy of the notice of appeal had not been sent "forthwith" within the meaning of r. 132.

Regina v Lloyd
Court of Criminal Appeal [1967] 1 QB

REGINA v LLOYD
COURT OF CRIMINAL APPEAL [1967] 1 QB

Crime - Homicide - Diminished responsibility - Summing up - Evidence that impairment of mental responsibility more than minimal - Whether "substantially" impaired - Jury directed that substantially not total and not trivial or minimal - Whether misdirection - Homicide Act, 1957 (5 & 6 Eliz. 2, c. 11), s. 2 (1).

The defendant was charged with the murder of his wife by strangling her in the early hours of January 1, 1965. At the trial he pleaded diminished responsibility under Section 2 (1) of the Homicide Act, 1957. According to medical evidence the defendant was suffering from mental abnormality, but none of the doctors for the defence would go so far as to say that his mental abnormality substantially impaired his mental responsibility, although all of them said that his mental responsibility was impaired to some extent, and that it was not minimal. The trial judge, summing up, directed the jury that the word "substantially" did not mean total, that the mental responsibility need not be totally impaired and that it was for the jury to say, on the evidence, whether the defendant's mental responsibility was impaired, and, if it was, whether it was substantially impaired. He went on to say that, if the jury found that the defendant's mental responsibility was substantially impaired, they should return a verdict of manslaughter and not a verdict according to the indictment. The jury convicted the defendant and he appealed, contending that "substantially" in Section 2 (1) of the Act of 1957 meant more than trivial and that as the evidence was that the impairment of mental responsibility was more than trivial, the defence was made out:

Held: dismissing the appeal, that there was no ground for criticism of the trial judge's direction, for the word "substantially" in Section 2 (1) must be given proper weight; and that it was for the jury to decide, looking at the evidence in a broad common-sense way, whether they thought the impairment of mental responsibility was substantial.

REGINA (RESPONDENT) AND SHEPPARD AND ANOTHER (APPELLANTS) HOUSE OF LORDS [1981] AC

Children and Young Persons - Offences against - Wilful neglect - Failure to provide necessary medical aid - Whether absolute offence - Children and Young Persons Act 1933 (23 & 24 Geo. S, c. 12), s. 1

By Section 1 of the Children and Young Persons Act 1933:

"(1) If any person who has attained the age of 16 years and has the custody, charge, or care of any child or young person under that age, wilfully ... neglects ... him ... in a manner likely to cause him unnecessary suffering or injury to health ... that person shall be guilty of a misdemeanour ... (2) For the purposes of this section - (a) a parent or other person legally liable to maintain a child or young person shall be deemed to have neglected him in a manner likely to cause injury to his health if he has failed to provide adequate ... medical aid ..."

A child 16 months old died of hypothermia and malnutrition; for some days previously he had suffered from gastroenteritis and vomiting and had been unable to ingest food. Though timely medical attention might have saved his life his parents, who were poor and also of low intelligence, did not realise that he was ill enough to require examination by a doctor. On their trial for neglecting the child, contrary to Section 1 (1) of the Act of 1933 the judge directed the jury that the test of their guilt was objective only, viz., whether a reasonable parent, with knowledge of the facts known to these parents, would appreciate that failure to have the child examined was likely to cause him unnecessary suffering or injury to health. They were convicted and the Court of Appeal upheld the convictions.

On appeal: -

Held:
allowing the appeal (Lord Fraser of Tullybelton and Lord Scarman dissenting), that to convict of the misdemeanour of neglecting to

provide adequate medical aid for a child contrary to the provisions of the Act the jury had to be satisfied

(a) that the child did in fact need medical aid at the time the defendant was charged with failing to provide it and

(b) either that the defendant was aware at that time that the child's health might be at risk if medical aid were not provided or that the defendant's unawareness of that fact was due to his not caring whether the child's health was at risk or not,

that had the jury been so directed it was not certain that they would have convicted one or both of the appellants and accordingly, the appeals would be allowed (post, *pp. 404 - 405A, 408E-F, 412A-C, 418D-E*).

RICE v CONNOLLY
DIVISIONAL COURT [1966] 2 QB

Police - Obstruction - Refusal to give name and address - Noncompliance with constable's request to accompany him to police box - Whether "wilful" obstruction - "Obstructs" - Police Act, 1964 (c. 48), s. 51 (3).

The defendant appeared to a police constable to have been acting suspiciously in an area where there had been a number of break-ins during the same night. He was asked several times for his full name and address, which he refused to give, and when asked to accompany the police constable to a police box, declined to do so, unless arrested. The defendant was convicted of wilfully obstructing the police constable in the execution of his duty, contrary to Section 51 (3) of the Police Act, 1964.

On appeal:

Held:
allowing the appeal, that "obstructs" in Section 51 (3) of the Police Act, 1964, meant the doing of any act which made it more difficult for the police to carry out their duty, and "wilful" meant not only "intentional" but without lawful excuse; that while every citizen had a moral or social duty to assist the police, there was no such legal duty, and the defendant in refusing to answer the police constable's questions (as opposed to telling a lie) or to accompany him to the police box was within his rights at common law; and that, therefore, the defendant had not "wilfully" obstructed the police constable, notwithstanding that the police constable was acting in the execution of his duty and that the defendant had made it more difficult for the constable to carry out his duty.

Per Lord Parker CJ There is all the difference between deliberately telling a false story - which a citizen has no right to do - and preserving silence - which he has every right to do (post, *p. 420A*).

Abdul Wahab Mohamed Sameen (Appellant) v Palliyaguruge Vithanage Sumana-Wathie Abeyewickrema and Others (Respondents)
On appeal from the Supreme Court of Ceylon
Privy Council [1963] AC

ABDUL WAHAB MOHAMED SAMEEN (APPELLANT) v PALLIYAGURUGE VITHANAGE SUMANA-WATHIE ABEYEWICKREMA AND OTHERS (RESPONDENTS)
ON APPEAL FROM THE SUPREME COURT OF CEYLON
PRIVY COUNCIL [1963] AC

1963 April 3
LORD DILHORNE LC, LORD EVERSHED, LORD JENKINS, LORD GUEST and SIR MALCOLM HILBERY

Ceylon - Practice - Appeal - Security for costs - Non-compliance with statutory requirements - Abatement of appeal - Statutory discretion to grant relief - In respect of "any" mistake, omission or defect - Notice of security to be lodged 'forthwith" - Meaning of 'forthwith" - Civil Procedure Code (legislative Enactments of Ceylon, 1956, c. 101), ss. 366, 756 (1) (3).

By Section 756 of the Civil Procedure Code of Ceylon: "(3) In the case of any mistake, omission, or defect on the part of any appellant in complying with the provisions of this section, the Supreme Court, if it should be of opinion that the respondent has not been materially prejudiced, may grant relief on such terms as it may deem just."

Judgement for the plaintiffs, the respondents, having been given in the District Court of Colombo on a Friday, the defendant, the appellant, filed a petition of appeal in that court on the following morning, Saturday, and pursuant to the provisions of Section 756 (1) read with Section 356 of the Code the appellant, when his petition of appeal was received by the court was required "forthwith" to lodge a notice of security for the respondents' costs of appeal with that court for the necessary steps to be taken for service of the notice by the Fiscal on the respondents. The notice of security was in fact filed on the following Monday. On a contention by the respondents in the District Court that the appellant's notice of security was bad in that it had not been filed with the court "forthwith" upon the petition of appeal being received by the court, that court forwarded the appeal to the Supreme Court who, treating the notice lodged on the

Monday as filed too late, upheld the respondents' contention. On appeal to the Board it was contended by the respondents, and conceded by the appellant, that the notice of Monday had not been filed for the purpose of complying with Section 756 to secure service by the Fiscal:

Held: that "forthwith" should not be construed as meaning "on the same day." The notice of security for costs could be filed "forthwith" even though not filed on the same day as the petition of appeal was received. "Forthwith" connoted that the notice must be filed as soon as practicable, but that must depend on the circumstances of each case.

Dictum of Soertsz J in *De Silva v Seenathumma* (1940) 41 NLR 241 at 249 disapproved.

Since, however, the procedure prescribed by Section 756 had not been complied with, the appeal, unless the appellant was granted relief under Subsection (3) of Section 756, was abated. That subsection applies to all the provisions of the section, and is also expressed to apply in relation to any mistake, omission or defect. The Supreme Court is given by the subsection the power to grant relief on such terms as it may deem just where there has been a failure to comply with an essential requirement of the section, subject to the limitation that it has not power to do so unless it is of the opinion that the respondent has not been materially prejudiced.

Dicta of Fisher CJ in *Silva v Goonesekere* (1929) 31 NLR 184 at 185, and of Soertsz J in *De Silva v Seenathumma,* 41 NLR 241 at 245 and 247 disapproved.

It did not follow that relief should be given even if the respondents had not been materially prejudiced, but relief should not be lightly withheld, for the effect of refusing relief might be to deprive a litigant of access to the Supreme Court and, if the original judgement was wrong, amount to a denial of justice. In the circumstances here the respondents could not have been materially prejudiced by the failure to file the notice of security with the court for service by the Fiscal and relief should be granted and the appeal not abated.

Judgement and decree of the Supreme Court of Ceylon (1960) 61 N.L.R. 442 reversed.

In the Court of Appeal [1910] 1 KB
Simmons v Heath Laundry Company

IN THE COURT OF APPEAL [1910] 1 KB
SIMMONS v HEATH LAUNDRY COMPANY

1910 Feb. 11, 15, 26
COZENS-HARDY MR, FLETCHER MOULTON and BUCKLEY LJJ

Employer and Workman - Compensation - Basis of Assessment - Concurrent Employment - Professional Services - "Workman" - "Contract of Service" - Workmen's Compensation Act, 1906 (6 Edw. 7, c. 58), s. 13; Schedule I, paragraph 1 (b), paragraph 2 (b).

A laundry girl, aged nineteen, had her hand injured by an accident arising out of and in the course of her employment. She earned *7s* a week at the laundry and she also gave piano lessons to a man's children at his house at *3s* a week. She applied under the Workmen's Compensation Act, 1906, that the latter sum might be taken into account under paragraph 2 (b) of the First Schedule in assessing the amount of compensation. The County Court judge held that as teacher of music she did not come within the definition of workman in the Act and awarded her *7s* a week compensation in accordance with paragraph 1 (b), proviso (b), of the First Schedule:

Held:
that the question whether an applicant in any particular case was a workman within the Act was a question of fact and that there was evidence to support the finding of the County Court judge.
The meaning of "contract of service" discussed.

STEVENS v BROMLEY LONDON BOROUGH COUNCIL [1967 S. No. 2497] COURT OF APPEAL [1972] Ch

1971 Nov. 11, 15, 16; Dec. 13 SALMON, EDMUND DAVIES AND STAMP LJJ

Town Planning - Caravan site - Use without planning permission - Caravan dwellers licensees of owner - Enforcement notice - Service on owner and licensees on different days - Whether licensees "occupiers" - Validity of notice - Town and Country Planning Act 1962 (10 & 11 Eliz. 2, c. 38), s. 45 (3) (a).

The plaintiff developed some land as a caravan site without planning permission. In February 1965 he sold a caravan to W and by the end of September 1965 had sold some ten caravans as permanent residences to caravan dwellers, each of whom paid the plaintiff £1.75 a week "rent." Each caravan was large with separate bedrooms, living room and bathroom. Main water, electricity and drainage were connected and many had gardens. On September 27, 1965, the local planning authority served an enforcement notice, under Section 45 of the Town and Country Planning Act 1962, on the plaintiff, as owner and occupier, requiring him, *inter alia*, to discontinue the use of the land as a caravan site. A copy of the notice had been served on W, as occupier, on September 25 and copies were served on the other caravan dwellers on various dates between the end of September and December. The notice was to take effect in each case at the expiration of 30 days of service.

The plaintiff sought a declaration that the notice was invalid, relying on *Bambury v Hounslow London Borough Council* [1966] 2 QB 204, since it had been served on owner and occupiers to take effect on different dates. The planning authority contended that the caravan dwellers were not occupiers but licensees, so that service on them was unnecessary. Plowman J found that the caravan dwellers were licensees but that in appropriate circumstances licensees could be "occupiers" within Section 45 (3) (a) of the Act of 1962[9]; and that in the circumstances the caravan dwellers were "occupiers" entitled to have the notice served upon them. He accordingly declared the enforcement notice invalid.

On appeal by the local planning authority, on the assumption (for the purposes of the present appeal) that *Bambury's* case was correctly decided:

Held:
Dismissing the appeal (Stamp LJ dissenting), that whether or not a person was an "occupier" within the meaning of Section 45 (3) (a) of the Town and Country Planning Act 1962 depended on the facts and circumstances of the particular case and, on the facts of the present case, including the fact that the caravans were permanent homes, the caravan dwellers although licensees, were "occupiers" of the plots on which their caravans stood and were entitled to be served with copies of the enforcement notice and that accordingly the notice, as served, was invalid.

Per Edmund Davies LJ A person living on a caravan site has no legal right to have an enforcement notice served on him unless he can establish a degree of control over and substantial duration of enjoyment of the premises concerned

[9] Town and Country Planning Act 1962, s 45 (3) (a)

SWALLOW v LONDON COUNTY COUNCIL
DIVISIONAL COURT [1916] 1 KB

1915 Dec. 10
RIDLEY, LUSH, and LOW JJ

Weights and Measures - Coal - Refusal by Carman to assist in weighing Coal - "Obstructing of the weighing" - Weights and Measures Act, 1889 (52 & 53 Vict. c. 21), s. 27.

Under s. 27 of the Weights and Measures Act, 1889, the person in charge of a vehicle in which coal is carried is under no obligation to weigh or assist in weighing the coal carried in the vehicle. The mere refusal, therefore, by him to assist in weighing the coal, although required to do so by an officer of the local authority, does not constitute an obstruction of the weighing within sub-s. 2 of s. 27.

Wheat (Appellant) and E. Lacon & Co Ltd (Respondents)
House of Lords [1966] AC

WHEAT (APPELLANT) AND E. LACON & CO LTD (RESPONDENTS) HOUSE OF LORDS [1966] AC

1965 Dec. 13, 14, 15, 16
VISCOUNT DILHORNE, LORD DENNING

1966 Feb. 15
LORD MORRIS OF BORTH-Y-GEST, LORD PEARCE and LORD PEARSON

Occupiers' Liability - "Occupation" - Inn - Manager employed by owners of inn - Manager's wife allowed to take in paying guests in private part of premises - Right of owners to enter private part for specific purposes - Paying guest killed by fall on staircase in private part - Whether owners in "occupation" - Whether any duty of care owed - Whether in breach of duty - Occupiers' Liability Act, 1957 (5 & 6 Eliz. 2, c. 31), ss. 1, 2.

Occupiers' Liability - Common duty of care - Inn - Paying guest killed by fall on staircase - Staircase left unlighted by manager - Standard of care - Liability of owners of inn - Occupiers' Liability Act, 1957, ss. 1, 2.

Negligence - Contributory negligence - Duty owed by injured party - Descending staircase in dark - Duty to act carefully - Death of injured party - Whether contributory negligence.

Court of Appeal - Fact, question of - Appeal from lower court - Duty of appellate court to decide what inference should be drawn from undisputed evidence - Fall down stairs in dark - Cause of fall.

The defendants, who were brewers, were the owners of a public-house the management of which they entrusted to a manager (who was also the licensee) employed by them under a service agreement. The agreement required him to carry on the business of selling the defendants' drinks on their behalf in the licensed portion of the premises (the ground floor) and to comply with their directions in relation to that business. He was to allow the defendants to enter the premises for the purpose of viewing the state of repair, testing or inspecting the stocks and was not to part with possession of the premises or any part thereof.

Clause 7 provided:

"The manager shall and may so long as he shall continue in the service of the employers occupy the same public-house without paying any rent, rates, or taxes for the same but shall quit ... immediately upon ceasing to be employed by the employers or at any time on receiving 28 days' notice in writing. ... Such occupation shall not ... create any tenancy as between the parties hereto nor give the manager any estate or interest in the premises."

There was no direct access between the licensed premises on the ground floor and the living accommodation on the first floor. There was a separate entrance through a door marked "Private" which opened onto a staircase leading to the first floor. There was also a back staircase from the first floor, at the bottom of which there was a door opening onto a back yard, which gave access to the serving area behind the bars. The defendants allowed the manager's wife, as a privilege, to take in paying guests in the upper part of the premises.
The plaintiff and her husband were staying in the private part of the premises as paying guests of the manager's wife. At about 9 p.m. on September 4, 1958, the husband left the plaintiff on the first floor to go to buy some drinks from the bar. He was subsequently found at the foot of the back staircase with a fractured skull from which he died. There was an electric light at the top of the staircase but there was no bulb in it at the time of the accident. There was also a handrail down the left-hand side of the staircase terminating directly above the third step.
The plaintiff brought an action under the Fatal Accidents Acts, 1846 - 1908, and the Law Reform (Miscellaneous Provisions) Act, 1934, against the defendants for damages in respect of her husband's death, alleging negligence and breach of duty under the Occupiers' Liability

Act, 1957. Winn J found that the probability was that the deceased fell from about the third step and was caused to fall by the fact that his hand which he had been running along the handrail came to the end of it. He probably stepped out with confidence thinking he had come to the bottom of the stairs. He found that there were two concurrent causes of the fall, the fact that the handrail did not extend to the foot of the stairs and "the absence of any light." Winn J held that the defendants were in occupation of the back staircase and therefore owed the common duty of care under the Occupiers' Liability Act, 1957, but that they were not in breach of any duty

1 Occupiers' Liability Act, 1957, s. 1: "(1) The rules enacted by the two next following sections shall have effect, in place of the rules of the common law, to regulate the duty which an occupier of premises owes to his visitors in respect of dangers due to the state of the premises or to things done or omitted to be done on them. (2) The rules so enacted shall regulate the nature of the duty imposed by law in consequence of a person's occupation or control of premises and of any invitation or permission he gives (or is to be treated as giving) to another to enter or use the premises, but they shall not alter the rules of the common law as to the persons on whom a duty is so imposed or to whom it is owed; and accordingly for the purpose of the rules so enacted the persons who are to be treated as an occupier and as his visitors are the same ... as the persons who would at common law be treated as an occupier and as his invitees or licensees. ..."

S. 2: "(1) An occupier of premises owes the same duty, the 'common duty of care,' to all his visitors, except in so far as he is free to and does extend, restrict, modify or exclude his duty to any visitor or visitors by agreement or otherwise. (2) The common duty of care is a duty to take such care as in all the circumstances of the case is reasonable to see that the visitor will be reasonably safe in using the premises for the purposes for which he is invited or permitted by the occupier to be there." Since the staircase was only dangerous if not lit and they could not reasonably foresee that the manager or his wife would have left it unlighted, he dismissed the plaintiffs claim. The Court of Appeal (Sellers LJ dissenting) held that since the defendants had precluded themselves from entering the private part of the premises (except for certain specific purposes) they were not in occupation of the premises and therefore did not owe the common duty of care in respect of the back staircase. On the plaintiff appeal:

Held:
that the defendants were in occupation of the first floor of the premises for the purposes of the Occupiers' Liability Act 1957, and owed the plaintiff and her husband the common duty of care; but that there was no evidence of any breach of that duty and, accordingly, the appeal failed .

Per Lord Denning, Lord Morris of Borth-y-Gest, Lord Pearson and Lord Pearce. Two persons may be occupiers of the same premises at the same time and both be under a duty of care to visitors.

Per Viscount Dilhorne. There being no dispute as to the primary facts and no direct evidence as to the cause of the fall it is the duty of the appellate court to evaluate the evidence and to decide what inference, if any, can be drawn from the undisputed evidence. The evidence was not sufficient to enable any deduction to be made as to the probable cause of the fall. *Benmax v Austin Motors Ltd* [1955] AC 370; [1955] 2 WLR 418; [1955] 1 All ER 326, HL (E) applied.

Per Viscount Dilhorne. The defendants did not, by their service agreement with the manager, divest themselves of the occupation of any part of the public-house. The agreement did not distinguish between one part of the premises and another and it was not right to infer it from the facts. The manager occupied the premises as a servant on behalf of the defendants and not on his own account.

Dicta of Tindal CJ in *Dobson v Jones* (1844) 5 Man. & Gr. 112, 120; *Glasgow Corporation v Johnstone* [1965] AC 609; [1965] 2 WLR 657; 1 All ER, 730, HL (Sc) and *Tennant v Smith* [1892] AC 150; 8 TLR 434, HL (Sc) applied.
Per Lord Denning. No guidance is to be obtained from the use of "occupier" in other branches of the law (post, *p. 577F*). The test in

Wheat (Appellant) and E. Lacon & Co Ltd (Respondents)
House of Lords [1966] AC

Salmond on Torts, 14th ed. (1965), p. 372, that an occupier is "he who has the immediate supervision and control and the power of permitting or prohibiting the entry of other persons" is too narrow. There are other people who are occupiers even though they do not say "Come in." If a person has any degree of control over the state of the premises it is enough.

Per Lord Morris of Borth-y-Gest. It may be that the extent of the particular control which is exercised within the sphere of joint occupation will become a pointer as to the nature and extent of the duty which reasonably devolves on a particular.

Per Lord Pearson. The foundation of occupier's liability is occupational control, i.e., control associated with and arising from the presence in and use of or activity in the premises. Duncan v Cammell Laird & Co Ltd [1943] 2 All ER 621 applied.

Section 2 (9) Access to Neighbouring Land Act 1992 – Unreasonable respondents ordered to pay applicant's costs. Applicant only ordered to pay cost of one meeting between respondents and their Solicitors.

WHEELDON v BURROWS [1879]
12 ChD 31

In 1856 and 1857 a Mr. Allen purchased two pieces of land. The land of the plaintiff which was part of the land purchased was divided from the remainder of the land by a wall. Mr. Allen constructed a shed/workshop close to the wall in 1858 and it was illuminated by skylights only. In 1861 Mr. Allen raised the wall and roof, and replaced the skylights with four new windows inserted into the wall. Later Mr. Allen constructed a millwrights shop which blocked one of the four windows and left three to provide illumination. This new structure was situated on land sold on by Mr. Allen in 1867. The land was resold and ultimately purchased by William Wheeldon who bought at auction in 1875 for £200. William Wheeldon's widow was the plaintiff.

In 1878 Mrs. Wheeldon erected hoardings which blocked the remaining windows in order to assert the uncontrolled use and possession of her land. The defendant demolished them in order to continue to receive light to the three remaining windows.

The defendant pleaded that the two properties had been sold at about the same time with the same terms and conditions and the right of light to the windows was expressly or impliedly reserved. The Vice-Chancellor ruled that the plaintiff was entitled to an injunction because the conveyance to her predecessor in title had been without any such reservation and that she could obstruct the light.

The defendant appealed. The appeal was dismissed. When land is in one ownership no easement can exist but a quasi easement may exist. Such a quasi easement would be the use of one part of the land for the benefit of another. For example, to drain one part into a sewer in another part. If an easement is intended to be granted on sale it must be granted expressly in the contract of sale.

WOODCOCK AND ANOTHER v SOUTH WESTERN ELECTRICITY BOARD [1975 W. No. 0280] QUEEN'S BENCH DIVISION: BRISTOL [1975] 1 WLR

1975 Jan. 27
DUNN J

Electricity - Supply - Occupier of premises - Squatters in occupation without knowledge or consent of owners - Electricity supply to premises cut off by electricity authority - Whether duty on authority to supply electricity - Whether squatters "occupier of any premises" Electric Lighting (Clauses) Act 1899 (62 & 63 Viet. c. 19), s. 27 (1)

The plaintiffs were squatters who had unlawfully occupied two adjoining premises without the knowledge or consent of the owners. The defendants were the electricity authority for the area. The plaintiffs' application for the supply of electricity was accepted by the defendants who supplied electricity to the premises for a period of two months. Thereafter, on discovering the plaintiffs' method of entry into, and the nature of their occupation of, the premises, the defendants cut off the electricity supply to the premises. The plaintiffs brought an action for a mandatory injunction to require the defendants to reconnect electricity to the premises pursuant to their duty to supply electricity to the "occupier of any premises" under Section 27 (1) of the Electric Lighting (Clauses) Act 1899.'

On the plaintiffs' summons for an interim injunction in the same terms:-

Held:

dismissing the summons, that "occupier" in Section 27 (1) of the Act of 1899 did not include a person whose original entry upon premises was unlawful and forcible; and that the defendants were entitled to discontinue the supply of electricity to the premises as they were under no duty to provide the plaintiffs with electricity.

Yewens, Appellant: Noakes, Respondent.
Court of Appeal 6 QBD

YEWENS, APPELLANT: NOAKES, RESPONDENT
COURT OF APPEAL 6 QBD

1880 March 16
BRAMWELL, THESIGER and BAGGALLAY, LJJ

Revenue - Inhabited House Duty - Exemption - "Servant or other Person" - 32 & 33 Viet. c. 14, s. 11.

The respondent was a hop-merchant, and was possessed of certain houses having an internal communication throughout, and used for the purposes of his trade. K. lived in the houses in order to take care of them, but he was a clerk in the respondent's employ at a salary of £150 a year, and he resided in the houses together with his wife, children, and servant:

Held,

that K. was not "a servant or other person" within the meaning of 32 & 33 Vict. c. 14, s. 11, and that the respondent was not exempt from inhabited house duty in respect of the houses.

The Access to Neighbouring Land Act (1992) Handbook

Table of Statutes

Appendix 1

Access to Neighbouring Land Act 1992

S 1(1)	65
S 1(1)(a)	65
S 1(1)(b)	65
S 1(2)(a)	65
S 1(2)(b)	66
S 1(3)	66
S 1(3)(a)	66
S 1(3)(b)	66
S 1(4)(a)	66
S 1(4)(b)	66
S 1(4)(c)	66
S 1(4)(d)	67
S 1(5)	67
S 1(5)(a)	67
S 1(5)(b)	67
S 1(6)	67
S 1(7)	67
S 1(7)(a)	68
S 1(7)(b)	68
S 1(7)(c)	68
S 2(1)	68
S 2(1)(a)	68
S 2(1)(b)	68
S 2(1)(c)	68
S 2(2)	68
S 2(2)(a)	69
S 2(2)(b)	69
S 2(3)	69
S 2(3)(a)	69
S 2(3)(b)	69
S 2(3)(c)	69
S 2(3)(d)	69
S 2(4)	69
S 2(4)(a)	69
S 2(4)(a)(i)	69
S 2(4)(a)(ii)	69
S 2(4)(b)	70
S 2(4)(c)	70
S 2(5)	70
S 2(5)(a)	70
S 2(5)(b)	70
S 2(6)	70

Table of Statutes

Access to Neighbouring Land Act 1992

S 2(6)(a)	70
S 2(6)(a)(i)	70
S 2(6)(a)(ii)	71
S 2(6)(b)	71
S 2(6)(b)(i)	71
S 2(6)(b)(ii)	71
S 2(7)	71
S 2(7)(a)	71
S 2(7)(b)	71
S 2(7)(c)	71
S 2(6)(b)(ii)	71
S 2(8)	71
S 2(8)(a)	71
S 2(8)(b)	72
S 2(8)(c)	72
S 2(9)	72
S 2(9)(a)	72
S 2(9)(b)	72
S 3(1)	72
S 3(2)	72
S 3(2)(a)	72
S 3(2)(b)	72
S 3(2)(c)	73
S 3(3)	73
S 3(3)(a)	73
S 3(3)(b)	73
S 3(3)(c)	73
S 3(4)	73
S 3(4)(a)	73
S 3(4)(b)	73
S 3(5)	74
S 3(5)(a)	74
S 3(5)(b)	74
S 3(6)	74
S 3(7)	74
S 4(1)	74
S 4(1)(a)	74
S 4(1)(b)	75
S 4(2)	75
S 4(3)	75
S 4(3)(a)	75
S 4(3)(b)	75
S 4(4)	75
S 5(1)	76
S 5(2)	76
S 5(2)(i)	76
S 5(3)	76

Access to Neighbouring Land Act 1992

S 5(4) 76
S 5(4)(a) 76
S 5(4)(b) 76
S 5(5) 77
S 5(6) 77
S 6(1) 77
S 6(1)(a) 77
S 6(1)(b) 77
S 6(1)(c) 77
S 6(2) 78
S 7(1) 78
S 7(2) 78
S 7(3) 78
S 8(1) 79
S 8(2) 79
S 8(3) 79
S 9(1) 80
S 9(2) 80
S 9(3) 80

Appendix 2

S 62 The Law of Property Act 1925

S 62 (1) 81
S 62 (2) 81
S 62 (3) 81
S 62 (4) 82
S 62 (5) 82
S 62 (6) 82

Appendix 3

Extracts from the Law Commission Report No. 151 on Rights of Access to Neighbouring Land

Improvements and alterations 83

4.8 83

Demolition and rebuilding 83

4.9 83
4.10 84

Demolition and rebuilding – continued

4.11 84

Non-structures 85

4.12 85

Ancillary 85

4.13 85

General power to make conditions 86

4.28 86
4.28 (a) 86
4.28 (b) 86
4.28 (c) 86

Making good 86

4.30 86
4.31 87

Compensation for physical damage 87

4.50 87

New respondents 87

4.74 87
4.75 88

Variation etc. 89

4.76 89

Jurisdiction 89

4.88 89
4.89 89
4.90 89
4.91 90
4.92 90
4.93 90

The effect of the order 91

4.106 91

Trespass ab initio[10] 92

4.111 92

Appendix 4

Order 49 – Rule 1 of the County Court Supplementary Rules (information to be included in an application) 93

(1) 93
(2) 93
(3) 93
(3)(a) 93
(3)(b) 93
(3)(c) 93
(3)(d) 93
(3)(e) 93
(3)(f) 93
(4) 94
(5) 94
(6) 94
(7) 94

[10]From the beginning

Table of Cases

ATKINSON v BETTISON [Plaint No. K. 737]
COURT OF APPEAL [1955] 1 WLR 135

BAKER v ELLISON
DIVISIONAL COURT [1914] 2 KB 137

BEWLAY (TOBACCONISTS) LTD v BRITISH BATA
SHOE CO LTD [Plaint No. N. 1690]
COURT OF APPEAL [1959] 1 WLR 139

BOMFORD (APPELLANT) v
OSBORNE (INSPECTOR OF TAXES) (RESPONDENT)
HOUSE OF LORDS [1942] AC 141

COULTON v PICKLES 1995 116

MICHAEL DEAN v GEORGE DOYLE WALKER
[1996] EWCA 380 113

DUNNING v UNITED LIVERPOOL HOSPITALS'
BOARD OF GOVERNORS [1972 D. No. 2591]
COURT OF APPEAL [1973] 1 WLR 143

ENGLISH CLAYS LOVERING POCHIN & CO LTD
v PLYMOUTH CORPORATION [1972 E. No. 1038] 146

FAWCETT PROPERTIES LTD (APPELLANTS) v
BUCKINGHAM COUNTY COUNCIL (RESPONDENTS)
HOUSE OF LORDS [1961] AC 148

FRANKLIN v THE GRAMOPHONE COMPANY, LIMITED
COURT OF APPEAL [1948] 1 KB 151

GRANADA THEATRES LTD v
FREEHOLD INVESTMENTS (LEYTONSTONE) LTD
CHANCERY DIVISION [1958] 1 WLR 152

GREEN v MOORE
DIVISIONAL COURT [1982] QB 154

HARRIS v BIRKENHEAD CORPORATION & ANOTHER
PASCOE AND ANOTHER THIRD PARTY
ALLIANCE ASSURANCE CO LTD FOURTH PARTY
[1970 H. No. 278] COURT OF APPEAL 1 WLR 156

Table of Cases

In re HATCHEK'S PATENTS
Ex parte ZERENNER
CHANCERY DIVISION [1909] 2 Ch 158

HILLINGDON LONDON BOROUGH COUNCIL
v CUTLER
COURT OF APPEAL [1968] 1 QB 161

HINCHLIFFE v SHELDON
QUEEN'S BENCH DIVISION [1955] 1 WLR 165

Ex parte LAMB. In re SOUTHAM.
COURT OF APPEAL 19 ChD 166

JACKSON (RESPONDENT) v
HALL AND ANOTHER(APPELLANTS)
WILLIAMSON (APPELLANT) v
THOMPSON AND ANOTHER (RESPONDENTS)
HOUSE OF LORDS [1980] AC 167

JONES v SCULLARD.
QUEEN'S BENCH DIVISION [1898] 2 QB 170

METHUEN-CAMPBELL v WALTERS
COURT OF APPEAL [1978] 247 EG 899 171

MILLER v OWNERS OF THE SHIP OTTILIE
COURT OF APPEAL [1944] 1 KB 175

MILLS & ROCKLEYS LIMITED v LEICESTER
CITY COUNCIL
KING'S BENCH DIVISION [1946] 1 KB 176

In re MUSCOVITCH. Ex parte MUSCOVITCH.
COURT OF APPEAL [1939] Ch 177

REGINA v LLOYD
COURT OF CRIMINAL APPEAL [1967] 1 QB 178

REGINA (RESPONDENT) AND SHEPPARD
AND ANOTHER (APPELLANTS)
HOUSE OF LORDS [1981] AC 179

RICE v CONNOLLY
DIVISIONAL COURT [1966] 2 QB 181

ABDUL WAHAB MOHAMED SAMEEN (APPELLANT) v.PALLIYAGURUGE VITHANAGE SUMANA-WATHIE ABEYEWICKREMA AND OTHERS (RESPONDENTS) ON APPEAL FROM THE SUPREME COURT OF CEYLON PRIVY COUNCIL [1963] AC 182

IN THE COURT OF APPEAL [1910] 1 KB
SIMMONS v HEATH LAUNDRY COMPANY 184

STEVENS v BROMLEY LONDON BOROUGH COUNCIL [1967 S. No. 2497]
COURT OF APPEAL [1972] Ch 185

SWALLOW v LONDON COUNTY COUNCIL
DIVISIONAL COURT [1916] 1 KB 187

WHEAT (APPELLANT) v
E. LACON & CO LTD (RESPONDENTS)
HOUSE OF LORDS [1966] AC 188

WHEELDON v BURROWS [1879] 12 ChD 31 193

WILLIAMS v EDWARDS AND EDWARDS [1997] CLYB 561 119

WOODCOCK AND ANOTHER v
SOUTH WESTERN ELECTRICITY BOARD
[1975 W. No. 0280]
QUEEN'S BENCH DIVISION: BRISTOL
[1975] 1 WLR 195

YEWENS, APPELLANT:
NOAKES, RESPONDENT.
COURT OF APPEAL 6 QBD 196

Index

Access Order 5, 15, 37, 45
  Anyone authorised to do work can apply 18
  Application for discharge of order 53-54, 58, 77
  Area to be entered 25, 29, 68, 93, 105
  Binds successors in title of servient land 19, 45-47, 74, 75
  Binds successors in title of dominant land 46
  Binds subsidiary interest in servient land 45, 47
  Consideration for right to enter 26, 33-5, 47, 70, 111, 116-118
  Dates works to be done 25, 29, 68, 91, 93
  Definition 61
  Discharge 51, 53, 57, 58, 76, 77, 89
  Drawing plans 31
  Effect of 37, 39, 72, 91
  Extends to anyone reasonably assisting 40, 85
  Extends to anything emanating from the work 23, 40, 85
  No automatic right 5, 18
  Overriding interest not acquired 52, 54, 77
  Period works to be done 5, 6, 25, 29, 37, 68, 107, 131
  Registration 46, 51-54, 76, 108
  Reinstatement 58
  Suspension 57, 58, 77, 89
  Terms and conditions 25, 26, 29, 30, 47, 68-9, 91, 127, 130, 133
  What shall be specified 25, 26, 29-31, 33, 43, 44, 62, 68-70, 94
  Where owner not identified 45-6, 74
  Works to be carried out 16-23, 30-32, 62, 66-8, 83-5, 111
Access to neighbouring land Act 1992 - in full 65
Advantage gained by appellant from
  access to servient land 27, 33, 34, 70, 107, 118-9
Adjustment, alteration or improvement to the land 17, 22, 67, 83
Agents 39, 74, 96, 97
All interested parties should be served with notice 18, 48
Allocation of proceedings 59, 78
Alteration, adjustment or improvement to the land 17, 22, 67, 83
Alterations for their own sake – not allowed 22, 83
Ancillary works of preservation 23
Applicant – definition 5, 46, 61, 75, 79, 96
Applicant's associates - definition 43, 74, 96
Applicant's financial advantage gained from access . . . 27, 29, 33, 34, 70
Application of The Act 57, 61, 77, 79
Application for
  discharge of order 53-54, 58, 77
  reinstatement of order 58
  suspension of order 57, 58, 77, 89
  variation of order 58, 131
Assessment of consideration 34
Associates 37-39, 43, 72-74, 96
Area of Servient land to be entered upon 25, 29, 68, 93, 105

Index

Bar on Contracting Out 45, 46, 48, 49, 74
Basic preservation works 16, 21, 33, 66, 67, 110
Branches from trees 40, 85
Breach of Terms and Conditions – damages for 39, 57, 58, 77, 133
Burden on applicant to prove necessity of works 20
Cables 16, 17, 41, 66, 68
Came into force 31st January 1993 . . . . 12, 63
Cannot be carried out without access 15, 20, 66, 104, 124
Cases
  brought under the Access to Neighbouring Land Act 1992 . . . . 113 ff.
  others which are relevant . . . . 135 ff.
"Catch all" section 8(1) 62
Caution 13, 51-54, 76-77
Checklists 103, 106, 108
Clearance 16, 66, 67
Common Law – no right of access 9
Compensation: 26, 32-34, 47, 69, 82, 86, 87, 89, 101, 106, 109, 110,
  . . . . 111, 116
  and commercial land 109, 111
  Cases under this provision of the ANLA 116
  County Court as Tribunal to determine quantum 89
  Expert to determine quantum 110
  Inconvenience 26, 32, 69
  Loss damage or injury 26, 32, 69, 87, 110
  Loss of privacy 26, 32, 69, 109
  Residential land 101
Condition schedule of servient land 26, 33, 42, 70, 109
"Connected with" 28, 35, 71
Consideration – assessment of 34
Consideration for entering onto servient land . 26, 33-5, 70, 111, 116-118
Contingency clause 62
Contracting Out – barred 45, 46, 48, 49, 74
Council of Mortgage Lenders Handbook 13
Court – the – definition 59, 61, 78, 79
Court's power to vary or exclude 38, 41, 42, 57, 73, 77, 89
Cutting back 16, 66
Damage 25, 26, 29, 30, 32, 33, 38, 41, 42, 44, 69, 70, 73, 84, 86
  . . . . 87, 93, 106, 108, 109, 110, 116, 117, 118, 125, 127, 128
Damaged 16, 67
Damages
  agreed in lieu of making good or removing rubbish 42
  contravention of or failure to comply with order 57, 58, 78
  for breach of Access Order 39, 57-58, 77-78, 133
  schedule of condition in claim for 33
Dates during which work may be carried out 26, 29, 68, 91, 93
Deemed consent for access 43, 91-92
Definitions 34, 62, 95-102
  Section 8 61
  Definition of residential land 28, 34, 71

Degree of inconvenience 27, 33, 70, 117
Demolition 17, 22, 67, 83, 84, 97, 116
Discharge 37, 51, 53-4, 57, 58, 73, 76, 77, 89
Discretion - court can exercise 21, 33, 47, 104, 110
Dispute – respondent should list any
matter which may give rise to a dispute 40
Disturbance 9, 15, 21, 49, 66, 104, 111, 129
Ditch 16, 67, 81, 85
Dominant land – definition 15, 61
Draft Bill 1991 12
Drain 16, 17, 66, 68, 81, 85
Drawing plans 17, 31, 68, 93, 105
Easements 7, 13, 81, 82, 91, 98, 115
Equitable easements 9
Implied right of access 8, 42
Interference with allowed 30, 62
London Building Acts 9
Lost Modern Grant 8
Express grant by deed 7
Presumed grant 8
Prescription – Prescription Act 1832 8
Quasi easements 9
Right of way 7, 9, 13, 62
Right of way of necessity 9
Statutory easements 9
Effect of Access Order 37, 39, 72, 91
Entry – Enter – construction of term 61, 79
Equipment 7, 23, 30, 37, 40, 72, 85, 88, 91, 103, 109
Exclusions – power of court to vary or exclude . 38, 41, 42, 57, 73, 77, 89
Expenses 28, 35, 72
Failed attempt at access – must be demonstrated 20
Felling 16, 66, 85
Financial advantage gained from access 27, 29, 33, 34, 70, 106
Giving of security by applicant 28, 35, 36, 72
Hardship 15, 21, 66, 104, 111, 114
Hedges 16, 66, 81, 85
History of the Act 11
Implied right of access 8, 42
Improvement , adjustment, or alteration to the land 17, 22, 67, 83
Improvement of dominant land 22
Incidentally 17, 22, 67
Inconvenience 21, 25-27, 29, 30, 32-35, 69, 70, 86,
. . . . 103-104, 107-109, 111, 116-118, 133
Indemnity 38, 73, 125
Information about servient land 19, 107, 121
Injury 25, 26, 30, 32, 33, 44, 69, 86, 93, 108, 110, 116, 125, 128
Inspections classed as work 17, 23, 68
Insurance 26, 33, 47, 70, 93, 106, 108, 125, 128
Interests created after making the Access Order 19, 45, 46, 47, 75

Index

Interference 15, 30, 49, 61, 62, 66, 79, 111, 129
Interpretation 61, 79, 95, 98, 115
Investigating servient land 19, 107, 121
Jurisdiction 59, 78, 82, 89, 90, 91
"Land" – excludes highway 61, 79, 98
Land Charges Act 1972 . . . . 45, 51, 52, 74, 76, 77
Land Registration Act 1925 . . . . 45, 51, 52, 53, 74, 76, 77
Land to be entered 25, 29, 68, 93, 105
Law Commissions Act 1965 11
Law Commission Report No 151 . . . . 12, 22, 83
Law Commission Working Paper No 78 . . 11, 12, 83, 85, 86, 87, 89, 92
Law of Property Act 1925 - s62 . . . . 8, 81
Licensee can apply for Access Order 18
Licensees bound 47
Lessees bound 47
London Building Acts 9
Loss of privacy 25, 26, 29, 30, 32, 33, 69, 86, 109, 116, 117, 118
Lost modern grant 8
Maintenance 8, 16, 20, 22, 66, 101, 103, 104, 108
Make good afterwards 37, 42, 73, 125
Manner in which works to be carried out 25, 30, 69
Map 17, 68, 105, 121, 122
Materials 23, 37, 40, 72, 85, 109, 125
Minimising disturbance 21, 29, 86, 103, 104, 108
Mortgagee's consent may not be required 19
Mortgagee in possession not bound by Access Order 19
Must be reasonably necessary 15-17, 20-25, 30, 37-39, 61, 65-69
. . . . 72-74, 79, 83, 88, 96, 104, 110-111, 114-115, 124
Name of respondent in application 18, 19, 45, 48, 75, 105, 106
Negligent conveyancing 13, 14
New building outside the Act 84
No right of access at Common Law 9
Nothing to be left on servient land on conclusion 38, 41, 74
Obstructive owner of servient land 39, 61, 79, 99
Onus on applicant to prove necessity 20, 110-111
Order 49 – Rule 1 of the County Court Supplementary Rules . . 48,93, 124
Order
- damages for breach 57, 77
- suspension of 57, 48, 77, 89
- variation of 38, 41, 42, 57, 58, 73, 77, 89, 131

Overriding interest not acquired 52, 54, 77
Owner not identified 45-46, 74
Pending land action 52, 54, 55, 77
Period during which work may be done . 5, 6, 25, 29, 37, 68, 72, 107, 131
Persons bound by Access Order 19, 45, 46, 47, 74, 88, 101
Persons "Connected with" the applicant 26-28, 32, 35, 39, 69, 70, 71
Persons who may carry out the work 26, 31, 35, 39, 69, 74
Physical damage 29, 86, 87
Pipe 9, 16, 17, 41, 66, 68, 95

Plan 17, 31, 68, 93, 105, 106, 119, 121, 122, 123, 124, 125
Plant and equipment 30, 37, 72, 106
Position prior to the Act 7
Power of court to vary or exclude 38, 41, 42, 57, 73, 77, 89
Power of entry 28, 39, 72, 74, 96
Precautions to be taken 26, 31, 69, 109, 127
Precedents . . . . 123 ff
Prescription Act 1832 8
Preservation of land 15, 16, 17, 20, 21, 22, 23, 61, 65, 66, 67, 68
. . . . 79, 83, 96, 101, 104, 110, 115, 124
Prior to the Act 8
Privacy - loss of 25, 26, 29, 30, 32, 33, 69, 86, 109, 116, 117, 118
Reasonably assisting 40, 85
Reasonably necessary: . . . .
    Preservation works 15, 16, 20, 22, 61, 66, 67
    For the preservation of land 15, 16, 17, 22, 23, 61, 65-68, 79, 83
. . . . 96, 104, 110, 111, 115, 124
Record condition 26, 33, 70, 109
Registration 51
    as pending land action 52, 54, 55, 77
    as writ or order 52, 54,55
    at Land Charges Registry or Land Registry 52, 53, 54
    discharge or cancellation 53-4, 55, 77
    Registered and Unregistered Land 52, 53, 54
    of notice or caution 52, 77
    without need for Land Certificate 51, 53, 76
Reimbursement 28, 35, 72
Reinstatement 41, 42, 58, 86, 109
Reinstatement on completion 41, 42,86, 109
Relief 57, 78, 82
Removal of waste 37, 38, 41, 42, 73, 74, 109, 125, 128
Renewal 16, 66
Repair 5, 8, 9, 11-13, 16, 20, 22, 29, 66, 83-84, 101-104, 107, 108
Report No 151 – Law Commission 12, 22, 83
Residential land 27, 28, 33, 34, 70, 71, 93, 101, 103
. . . . 103, 106, 108, 110, 111, 118, 124
Residential land – no consideration payable 27, 33
Residential land - definition 28, 34, 71
Respondent's right to object 21, 110, 111
Respondent
    should list any matter which may give rise to a dispute 40
    should ensure nothing foreign may remain after works 41
    Who to name in application 18, 19, 45, 48, 75, 105, 106
Restrictive covenants 30, 89
Right to object 21, 110, 111
Rights of way of necessity 9
Rights of way – interference with allowed 62
Royal Assent 16th March 1992 12
Rubble 23, 31, 40, 44, 85, 109, 125, 127

Index

Scaffolding 23, 108, 109, 116, 117, 119
Schedule of condition of servient land 26, 33, 42, 70, 109
Security for expenses 28, 35, 36, 72
Servants 39, 74, 101
Servient land . . . .
- Definition 61, 79, 101
- Successors in title bound by Access Order 19, 45-47, 74, 75
- To be reinstated 38, 41-42, 73, 86, 109
Sewer 16, 17, 66, 68, 81, 85
Short Title 63, 80
Shrubs 16, 66
Six carpenters case 43, 92
Specified works - definition 61, 79, 101
Statutory Undertaker can apply for Access Order 18
Steps to minimise disturbance 21, 103, 104
Substantially more difficult without access 15, 20, 66, 101-102, 104
Successors in title of dominant land 46
Successors in title of servient land bound by Access Order . 19, 45-7, 74-5
Superior interests in land 19
Suspension 57, 58, 77, 89
Terms and conditions of Access Orders 25-26, 29-30, 47, 68-69, 91
. . . . 127, 130, 133
The court - definition 59, 61, 78, 79
Those undertaking the work 18, 26, 31, 69
Times when work may be carried out 5, 6, 31, 32, 42
Tortious entry 43, 92
Treatment – trees, hedges or shrubs 16, 40, 66
Trees 16, 40, 66, 81, 85
Trespass` 7, 30, 38, 43, 74, 88, 92, 99, 102
Underlessees bound 47
Unidentified persons 45-46, 74
Unreasonable to make the order 16, 21, 66, 111, 114, 129
Use or enjoyment 15, 66
Value of compensation payable 26, 27, 32, 33, 34, 70, 117, 118
Variations 38, 41, 42, 57, 58, 77, 89, 131
Vary – court's power to vary or exclude 38, 41, 42, 57, 73, 77, 89
Waste arising from the work 37, 38, 73, 74, 109
Leaving on servient land 38, 41, 74
Nothing to be left after conclusion of works 41
Removal from servient land 37, 38, 41, 42, 73, 74, 109, 125, 128
Who can apply for an Access Order? 15, 18, 20, 28, 95-96
Who may carry out the work 26, 31, 43-4, 69, 108
Who should be served with notice? 18, 48
Working Paper No 78 – Law Commission . 11, 12, 83, 85, 86, 87, 89, 92
Workmen 18, 26, 31, 117, 119
Works must be reasonably necessary 15-17, 20-25, 37-39, 61, 65-69
. . . . 72-74, 79, 83, 88, 96, 104, 110-111, 114-115, 124
Works to residential land 27, 28, 34, 70, 101, 103, 118